WOUNDED WORKERS

Recovering from Heartache
in the Workplace and the Church

Kirk E. Farnsworth

WinePress Publishing
MUKILTEO, WA 98275

To Rosie

With her own hands she plants a vineyard . . .
She is energetic, a hard worker, and watches for bargains . . .
She sews for the poor, and generously gives to the needy.
(From Proverbs 31, **The Living Bible**)

[She is] a wife of noble character . . .
She is clothed with strength and dignity . . .
She speaks with wisdom, and faithful instruction is on her tongue.
(From Proverbs 31, **New International Version**)

Acknowledgments

I owe a special debt of gratitude to:

- My friends, fictitiously named for purposes of confidentiality, who graciously consented to have their stories included in this book.

- The countless Christian workers who, during consultations with their organizations, provided examples of woundedness.

- The many authors who greatly enriched my understanding of the variety of topics I have covered in this book, and whose excellent material I was able to adapt to Christian workers and their places of work and worship.

- The many colleagues who critiqued earlier versions of the manuscript and the numerous folks who greatly encouraged me during workshops for wounded workers.

- Susan Rose, who personally sacrificed to complete the typing of the manuscript in its many forms and who prayerfully upheld the entire project from beginning to end.

- Jim Peak, for his conscientious editorial assistance in making the book clear and concise.

- Craig and Kristi Farnsworth, whose professional and inspired rendering of the book cover made their father mighty proud.

- Muriel Farnsworth, for her loving desire to give financial support to her son's vision and to see it materialize.

Contents

Introduction

NO ORGANIZATION IS PERFECT. What you see is not what you get. Organizations have a natural tendency to advertise themselves one way and to act another.

For example, Christian schools and colleges advertise total commitment to biblical values and standards, yet faculty, students and parents find exceptions in actual practice. Non-Christian companies establish their reputation on highly principled marketing slogans and business practices, yet employees and customers find exceptions in actual practice. Parachurch organizations base their operational policies and procedures firmly on Christian principles, yet employees and donors find exceptions in actual practice. Churches thoroughly promote Christ-centered worship and programs, yet again, worshipers and workers find exceptions in actual practice.

Countless Christian and non-Christian organizations are looking good, like standing fields of ripening wheat. But throughout the fields are stalks that have no shoots and will produce no grain. These organizations have within them, using the prophet Hosea's phrase, "standing grain [that] has no heads."[1]

As an example, consider the area of church leadership. It may appear on the surface that the pastoral leadership of a particular church is a standing field of ripening wheat. But in many cases, some stalks are standing in the shadows of others. Ecclesiastical power is quenching the Spirit in those—especially women—who desire to truly worship and minister to others as they are gifted by the Holy Spirit. Pastors are letting into their churches only the light of their own reality, and the people are wilting. The stalks are bare.

Where do we look for correction? We live in a time of a leadership crisis, so it is proposed by many that we start with the leadership. They assume that leadership transformation precedes corporate transformation and that everything rises and falls on leadership. Thousands of books and seminars take this approach. Another school of thought emphasizes the fact that we also live in a time of organizational chaos. This puts the emphasis on the corporate culture and gives priority to the entire system rather than the individuals within the system. This is also a very popular approach.

These are both worthwhile approaches. However, they are limited in two ways. First, they ignore the wounds inflicted on the workers by dysfunctional leaders and organizations. At best, they offer indirect maneuvers to prevent further wounding of workers in the future. But they do not dress present wounds, and they do not address strategies for workers taking direct control of their vulnerability to being wounded in the future.

Second, with few exceptions, dysfunctional leaders and organizations are dealt with on an entirely human (psychological, sociological, economic) level. I am convinced that Christian organizations in particular ignore the spiritual dimension, at their own extreme peril. Changing organizational cultures and leaders is not a cure-all when structural and personal sin lurk in the background. Instead, strongholds must be broken to counter the destructive realities of the powers of darkness. We dare not underestimate the determination of the enemy to disrupt and distort God's work, even through His own people!

My first goal in this book is to direct attention beyond reengineering organizations and refocusing leaders to recovering workers. My passion is to help those whose lives have been wrecked by their work and who have been left to fend for themselves. My second goal is to fully integrate the human and spiritual aspects of the recovery process, so that wounded workers can truly be whole again.

This book is a recovery manual for wounded workers, with two caveats. First, it does not include areas of abuse that involve legal action and/or specialized therapeutic intervention, such as physical or sexual abuse. That is beyond the scope of this book. However, even in these areas, the information presented on the spiritual side will still be relevant. No realm of recovery should be restricted to human strife only. It always includes the possibility of spiritual warfare, at both the individual and the corporate level.

The second caveat is that this book has less relevance for people with wounds in the past than for people with wounds in the present. However, if a person has been wounded in the past, has moved on to another job or ministry, and has memories that have not healed, this book will do two things: It will provide tools to assess the realities of the situation that turned sour, and it will provide the truths that are necessary to put it all into proper perspective.

The purpose of this book is to acknowledge the hurt and to offer peace and a way to a future with hope.[2] It is a reliable guide for Christian workers in both Christian and secular organizations. The examples, however, are primarily from Christian organizations. This book is also a reliable guide for every person from management level on down. Perhaps you, whatever your station may be, feel battle weary or betrayed in your job. Perhaps you have been burned out or burned up by your church. For instance, has your pastor used the people in your church to serve his personal vision and justified the cost of flamed-out lives as the price of success? Or, are you deeply disappointed and upset over your organization not living up to its Christian name? Are you bothered by your organization's actions not being fully in accordance with biblical principles (not illegal, but irresponsible; not unethical, but unloving; not dishonest, but dishonoring)? Or, finally, are you struggling to live up to your own Christian name in a non-Christian organization? Are you being drawn into petty grievances and gossip, and becoming a poor witness for Christ?

Do you know people who are intimidated and threatened when they challenge unjust practices, or who are ignored when they simply question anything at all? Do you know people who feel they cannot be what God wants them to be and remain in the organization, or who have been so used and abused that they have just given up? Are you aware of any situations like the following one, which was reported in *Christianity Today* (CT)?

> From a variety of sources, the work atmosphere at [a well-known parachurch organization] has been characterized as unusually tense, stressful, and at times verbally abusive (CT, May 17, p. 74). Earlier this year CT obtained from a reliable source copies of ministry memos, which paint a stark picture of how [the president] deals with his workers . . . .
>
> People are scared they will be fired. The way [the president] treats his employees in such a browbeating manner, in a denigrating way, people start to doubt their own self-worth . . . . He is never to blame for anything the way he does business.[3]

In all of these situations, the common denominator is powerlessness in effecting positive and lasting change and helplessness in addressing deep personal hurt. For those in Christian organizations, the unstated message is: They thought it was a Christian organization, and look at what it is doing to them!

Wounded Workers begins at your point of woundedness. It helps you put words to your wound. It helps you accept the reality of the hurt that now has a name. And, it gives you guidelines for recovery. The context for recovery is systemic, involving the entire organization rather than the isolated individual. This differs significantly from the traditional view that these are individual matters that must be dealt with exclusively on an individual basis.

For example, workers who are perceived as disturbed or disruptive are customarily dealt with directly. Seen as irrational, they are indoctrinated. Seen as irresponsible, they are disciplined. Seen as incompetent, they are given performance evaluations. Seen as mentally or emotionally impaired, they are provided mental health interventions. In very few cases is the organization itself called into question or held accountable in any way.

In this book, organizations are held accountable. Organizations can be dysfunctional, just as individuals can be. This is an important point, because it allows wounded workers to gain a broader perspective of reality, from which they can frame the choices they must make in coping with their situation. Knowing there can be crazy places as well as crazy people allows them to remain sane in insane places.

Descriptions of dysfunctional organizations run from the ordinary to the extraordinary. The most common way to describe dysfunctional organizations is to make a list of signs and symptoms, such as "the system stifles creativity," "the organization cannot face its problems openly," "workers are constantly subjected to unwarranted stress," or "constructive suggestions are taken as personal criticisms."[4] Among the most unusual descriptions is the "incestuous organization." This is an organization that has become the sole arena for meeting members' personal as well as professional needs. It is a place where members are dominated by social control, emotional suffocation and intrusion into personal affairs.[5]

I have selected three major types of dysfunctional organizations: the *neurotic* organization, the *addictive* organization and the *spiritually abusive* organization. Each type will be discussed in a separate chapter. First, in examining neurotic organizations, you will have an opportunity to see how the personalities of the people involved in organizational leadership are a major contributing factor to the structural and cultural pathologies of their organizations. Second, in examining addictive organizations, you will learn that many processes that are thought to be acceptable organizational behavior are actually addictive behavior disguised as corporate structure and function. Finally, in examining spiritually abusive organizations, you will encounter a sad state of affairs in which spiritual manipulation and false spiritual authority create an inversion of the body of Christ—followers being coerced to meet the needs of the leaders. If you happen to work in a non-Christian organization, this chapter will prove to be more helpful in understanding spiritual realities than it will be in seeing applications to your situation.

In each of these three chapters, you will be given a series of questions to use as a tool to put your organization to the test. After completing these tests, you will be able to conclude whether your organization is neurotic, addictive, spiritually abusive or some combination of the three. In addition, you will be asked to put yourself to the test. Do you have personality characteristics and/or spiritual strongholds that you bring to the situation that make matters worse?

I have discovered three phases of the recovery process: *recognizing* what is, *remembering* what should be and *responding* to what can be done about it. When you have finished putting your organization and yourself to the test, you will have completed Phase One of your recovery. The next two chapters of the book move you through Phase Two. This is a pause in the process when it is imperative that you remember what should be. Take a moment to think about organizations and their leaders and workers. Ask yourself what a bottom-line issue is for each one. I have formulated three questions that I believe provide biblical reality checks for the fundamental issues. What is the ideal organization? What is servant leadership? What is my calling? In other words, what unchanging truths can a Christian worker hold on to when everything is in turmoil and nothing is as it should be?

Consider the first question: What would be your biblical vision of the ideal organization (Christian or non-Christian)—an organization that, if it existed, would relieve you of your pain? Having this vision does not in and of itself make things better, but it is much better than not knowing that something is wrong. Some would argue that it is much less frustrating to not know the difference or to at least not pay attention to it. They believe that ignorance is bliss. I would disagree. Sure, it can be frustrating to know how things could be different and to never see them change; but to have no alternative is to have no future. If it's the way it is, or nothing, there is no hope.

Then, consider the second question: What is the biblical perspective on servant leadership? Most Christians believe, and many non-Christians agree, that servant-style leadership is the best leadership model. In the ideal situation, everyone in the organization would exhibit the characteristics of servant leadership. This is an important concept, because if the designated leaders do not demonstrate servant leadership, I believe their behavior can be intentionally shaped by their followers. If followers fully understand and practice servant leadership themselves, they will often be able to shape their leaders' behavior—at least to some degree—in the same direction. They do this by showing appreciation for their leaders' servant-like behaviors, which encourages their repetition. Without sound biblical knowledge of servant leadership, however, the tendency will be to simply cast everything the leaders do in the negative, and the leaders will probably get worse.

The third question is the most fundamental for the Christian worker: What is the biblical perspective on *calling*? This provides the framework for everything that is happening in your situation. Biblically, career and calling are not the same thing. If you do not understand this, and you are a victim of downsizing or have been fired, then you will potentially be robbed of the motivation to move on to another job with hope and confidence. If you do not know your calling in the biblical sense of the term, then you will also be vulnerable to being defined as a person by the elements of your environment. Pressures that influence you to behave in un-Christlike ways could rob you of any impact you might be able to have in moving your organization and/or leader toward the biblical ideal.

Your number one job is to refuse to be compromised. You must remain true to your calling. You must keep your convictions in the midst of your torment. That is the key to the recovery process. And the hand that turns the key is the biblical reality check of your Christian identity and of your Christian ideals.

Phase Two of the recovery process, remembering what should be, is the wellspring for the other two phases. Without remembrance of biblical perspectives on the basic issues, the recognition of corporate and individual faults and appropriate response have no life. Without Phase Two, recovery is dead.

Phase Three awaits completion of Phases One and Two. Only then can you ask the question, "What can I do about it?" Only then are you firmly enough grounded in both the "I" and the "it" of the recovery process. Basically, the choice is between seeking relief within the situation and seeking release from the situation. Although there are only two possible outcomes (make the situation better or leave), there are three strategies. They are to carry the freight, to fight or to take flight.

The first option, to carry the freight, is *ministering to others* through abiding. This is actively taking on the weight of the situation and other workers' burdens and being a faithful witness to what God is calling you to and to what an organization should be like. It is not to be confused with staying in the situation while moving away from the conflict, passively waiting it out. Rather, abiding in this context has two active forms of engaging the conflict: entering into communion with the suffering of others, as a prophetic witness, or with the suffering of a specific other person, as a wounded healer.

While the first option, the freight option, is to bear with others' burdens, the second option, the fight option, is to bear down on others' faults. It is *making changes*. The success of this strategy depends entirely on knowing who the real enemy is. The apostle Paul did us a great favor by revealing to us the work of the Powers. These are spiritual manifestations in the form of organizational structures and human teachings and traditions and, while they bring order and stability to the organization, they also claim for themselves the status of idols. They separate us from the love of Christ.

The Powers do more than separate us from the lordship and love of Jesus Christ; they also create doorways of invitation for demonic agents to enter into individual and organizational activity and inflict bondage to demonic activity. I acknowledge that these are not the only battlefields of spiritual warfare. There are many of varying types. However, the main point is this: You are not fighting merely against flesh and blood. As an agent of change, you must undertake to reform dysfunctional people and also redeem the Powers and reclaim strongholds that have been exploited by satanic forces.

The third and final option is the final solution: flight, or *moving on*. With this choice, you come to the end of the recovery process.

Whether you have decided to quit for the sake of principle or for the equally valid reason of self-preservation, those two words, "I quit," are two of the most emotional words you'll ever say. Leave-taking can get extremely complicated. In deciding how to leave, you must decide if it is more important to make a statement or to exit with class—although the two options are not entirely mutually exclusive. Unfortunately, making a statement that will lead to change is usually a pipe dream. In contrast, leaving with class is always within your reach and should be the goal of every Christian worker.

In summary, Phase Three gives you the opportunity to choose among three options: abiding, working for change or leaving. And, if you choose the third option, you have another choice: to make a statement and leave with class, or to just leave with class. These are hard choices to make. To help you decide which course of action to take, a self-assessment—that pulls together pertinent information from previous chapters—has been included in each of the final three chapters of the book.

Whatever you do, act in love. And if you honor the Lord in the details, He will bless you. Through it all, my hope is that your wound will not be your dwelling place, and that your woundedness will not become your destiny.

PREPARING THE SOIL

Words of the
Wounded

"How can I go in there and teach? I've been fired!" Larry was weeping. He was devastated. He was as broken as anyone I have ever seen.

It was eight o'clock in the morning. What a crummy way to start the day. We had been doing this for a couple of weeks. Every morning we would carpool to the college and then sit in the car in the faculty parking lot. Every morning we would repeat the same sad routine, until Larry mustered the courage to go in and face his first class for the day.

What neither of us could understand was how a faithful member of a Christian college community, who had given fifteen years of service to the college, could be treated with such little respect. He had been summarily and unjustifiably let go—without warning and without explanation. He was to finish out the remaining month of the semester and then be gone.

Let me make it clear that the administration's action was not about Larry's morality or the quality of his performance as a teacher. It was about money. The college had to cut costs to survive. But Larry had to survive too. He was terrified at the thought that his father was fifty-three years old when he was fired from his job and died of a heart attack. Now Larry, too, was fifty-three and had just been fired. Was history going to repeat itself?

Larry's faith was shaken down to its very foundation. It was like a tree with its leaves falling off one by one. The first leaf to fall off was his faith in God's sovereign rule over Christian institutions. It was unbelievable that this could happen in a Christian institution. Next to fall was his faith in a college that called itself Christian. Surely, he had thought, they would not do things here like they do in secular institutions. Then his faith in people fell. Even if the institution's policies didn't save him, he thought, the people would. Someone would come to his rescue. And when no one did, the last leaf fell down: his faith in himself. He was unfit and unworthy. He was unnecessary and unwanted.

Why had this happened? In trying to understand, Larry naturally looked first to God. God is supposed to ensure things like love and justice in organizations that say they exist for the very purpose of reflecting God's character in all that they do. And he looked to the institution itself and the people in it with the hope that somehow love would be expressed and justice would be done. But when nothing happened to make things right and relieve him of his pain, he turned inward.

What happens when we turn inward? On our good days, perhaps we find remedies to the barrenness around us or relief from the unbearable pressures and stress that others bring into our lives. But on our bad days, we start looking for what is wrong with us. Why am I such a failure? What could I have done differently? I have nowhere to go. No one wants someone like me.

Larry did not have a heart attack, but fifteen years later he still did not have a full-time job. He just never fully recovered from being forced to lose faith in himself. We have kept in touch through the years, and I am pleased that Larry has regained his faith that God is indeed ultimately in control. In addition, he has a much more realistic view of human institutions, whether Christian or secular. He has rebounded in his relationships with others, slowly learning once again to trust and just be himself. But that deep, deep wound inside him is taking much longer to heal.

WOUNDED WOMEN IN THE CHURCH

I have a special place in my heart for wounded workers like Larry. I have worked in many kinds of organizations, secular and Christian, and have heard hundreds of stories of personal pain. As a naval officer, college professor, professional counselor, corporate executive and church elder, I have witnessed countless people trying to stay sane in insane places and struggling to function as Christians in dysfunctional places of both work and worship.

Especially close to me is the plight of wounded women in the church, women who feel unused or used up. As a result, they conclude that their church is polluted or even poisonous—tainted, if not downright toxic.[1] My wife, Rosie, and I have attended some churches through the years that we believe would, to some degree, qualify.

Rosie and I have found that one of the issues that is often associated with significant underlying problems is the issue of *what women cannot do*. It is one of those unspeakables that everyone knows but won't discuss as such. But its apparent effects can be far reaching. Over and over again, when a church narrowly defines women's gifts and limits their expression, we have found problems with the quality of worship, an increase in the incidence of spousal and sexual abuse within church families, marginal functioning and spiritual apathy within the church board, and serious relational problems within the pastor's family. I do not mean to imply causation from correlation, or, in other words, to suggest that the mistreatment of women necessarily causes these other problems. But I am saying that they do tend to appear together in the several dysfunctional churches that we have observed.

I vividly recall when the issue of what women cannot do in the church really hit home. We were living in New England. I was teaching at the University of New Hampshire, and we were attending a large Evangelical church. One evening I received a phone call from the chairperson of the church nominating committee. He asked if I would be interested in becoming the Sunday school superintendent. I said, "Well, I don't feel as qualified in administering other teachers as I do in actually being a teacher myself. And to be honest, I'm not really interested in that job. But my wife is qualified, and I'm sure she would like to have the job. Why don't you ask her?"

He said, "I'll have to call you back."

This is when it became really bizarre. He did call back, with this offer: The committee felt that since women should not hold that office, perhaps Rosie and I could be co-superintendents. Furthermore, since I was very busy with my university job, the work could be done by Rosie; and if anything needed to be announced from the pulpit, that could be done by me. In effect, I would take the credit. Their proposal was absolutely unthinkable.

It got worse. After going back to the drawing board and searching diligently but unsuccessfully for a man to take the job, the committee came up with the twisted idea of substituting another man for me as figurehead but continuing to use Rosie. And, for propriety, they would ask the other man's wife to act as a chaperone when the other man and Rosie needed to meet together.

How was Rosie feeling through all this? She was crushed—all those demeaning messages, not the least of which was that she could do the job if only she were a man. Qualifications were beside the point. Her tearful response was, "The only thing that would make the difference would be if I shaved in the morning!"

My response was from then on to refuse any church job that was not available to a qualified woman as well as a qualified man. It turned out that Rosie was finally given the job of Sunday school superintendent in that Evangelical church in New England, and she did an exemplary job and blazed a trail for all the other women in that church as well. But I will never forget her statement to the committee when they came back a final time in desperation to offer her the job: "I'm still a woman, you know."

I was wounded pretty deeply by seeing her go through that. All she wanted to do, from the very start of the whole thing, was to use her gifts as she was called to do: to serve God and to bring glory to Him. I must say that I am still keeping my word to willingly accept an assignment only if qualified women are also considered. For example, I will be happy to speak from the pulpit the very next week after the first woman does. True, I have not spoken much from pulpits, and I did not serve on a single church board for quite a few years. But I have been able to show little children kept in nurseries that they are important enough for both men and women to care of them. In addition, I have been able to show women kept in "their place," that they are important enough to participate in ministries that change lives, as well as diapers, and important enough to serve the Lord's Supper, as well as church suppers. (My point is not that one ministry is better than another, but that opportunity is better than restriction when there is a God-given call to a particular type of ministry.)

Another example that stands out in my mind occurred several years later, when we moved to Illinois for my appointment to the faculty of a Christian college. Along with the move came many hidden costs, as is usually the case. It was hard, but it was a great time of spiritual growth for our family, as we learned to utterly depend on the Lord to provide for us. Through it all, we never cut back on our giving. We continued to give proportionately, even sacrificially, out of my earnings. There were times when we literally did not know where the next meal would come from, but God always provided.

During this time, God was showing Rosie through Scripture, and showing us through her, the way He wanted us to live: plant, expect a harvest and give thanks. One way to give thanks is to give testimony of God's grace to other believers. And, since we were attending a Bible-believing church, with a fairly unstructured Sunday service with lots of sharing, that seemed like a likely place to do it.

Wrong. The leaders of the church proclaimed loudly and with one voice, "Women cannot teach men here." Then it got bizarre again. Rosie was allowed to take twenty minutes during an adult class one Sunday morning to share all that God was doing in our family's life. She shared Scripture, and several men and women later changed their behavior in the area of giving. For example, one young lady began giving regularly for the first time in her life. Yet, right after the class, one of the elders reminded her she had not been "teaching" that morning, because men were in the class!

We joined the kids and went to the worship service immediately following our classes. We sang, we gave praise to the Lord, and we broke bread together. Then it was time for the teaching part of the service, or the sermon. A young man, probably twenty years old, stood up, strode to the lectern and said, "As I was thinking last night about what I could speak on today, nothing came to me. So I thought about . . . ." We wept together.

Perhaps you, too, have wept over something that has quenched the Spirit in another person's life. Or perhaps you have experienced someone who has diminished your own personhood and what God has shown you, causing the activity of the Holy Spirit to be stifled in your life. You need to know that you are not alone, crazy or heretical. Instead, you are wounded.

WHAT ARE YOUR WOUNDS?

I cannot possibly describe everyone's woundedness. Some wounds are short lived, while some seemingly go on forever. Wounds differ in intensity and how they affect people. One person's wound is not another person's wound. In fact, one person's wound may not even seem like a wound to another person. But make no mistake about it: A wounded person is a hurting person. The wound is not like a stubbed toe or a toothache; the whole person hurts. Another point that I want to make is that the size of the wound or its intensity is not what matters, because the pain goes right to the heart. And the pain is real, equally real for everyone.

To help you begin to understand your wounds and put words to them, I have some questions. Read each one slowly and ponder how each of the italicized words applies to your place of work or to you personally.[2] Write out your own examples.

Is your situation:

- *Unbelievable*? Is it *unthinkable* and *unreal* that you have been forced to quit simply because you dared to question how things were being done or because of a personality conflict with your supervisor?

- *Unbearable*? Is it *unforgivable* to you that you were let go with indecently short notice, not allowed to give input before the decision was made, and not given any assistance in making post-employment adjustments?
- *Unjustifiable*? Do you feel it is *unfair* that you were taken off a church committee because your competence was a threat to the pastor?

Do you feel:

- *Unusable*? Do you feel *unfit*, *unworthy* and *uncalled* and that your spiritual gifts are going *undiscovered* because you are not allowed to express them?
- *Untouchable*? Do you feel *unwanted*, *unaccepted* and *unnecessary* because you point out that your organization (church, college, company, etc.) does not operate consistently in accordance with biblical principles?

Do you yearn to speak:

- The *unspeakable*? Do you wish you could discuss the *undiscussables*, those things that everyone knows about but is afraid to bring up—weaknesses of the boss or pastor, flaws in decision making, favoritism, poor or even illegal stewardship, *unethical* or *uncaring* personnel policies, or misplaced or inappropriate priorities?[3]

Fear of Repercussions

A recent study reports four primary reasons for not speaking up, for not speaking the unspeakable.[4] They are fear of repercussions, the conviction that nothing will change, a desire to avoid conflict, and reluctance to cause trouble for others. However, while these are all potential reasons, the study concludes that by far the most common reason is the fear of repercussions.

Repercussions are very real in the Christian world—too real. I have consulted through the years with Christian organizations—

churches, parachurches, colleges and companies—that have problems within their organizational culture. The climate they create produces insecurity, stagnation, and a great deal of discouragement among members and employees. In one such organization, I asked all of the employees to tell me what they were not talking about on the job (unspeakables) and why (feared repercussions). In summary, here is what they told me:

UNSPEAKABLES	REPERCUSSIONS
1. Management decision-making styles	1. Poor employee performance evaluation
2. Employee's personal problems and job-related stress	2. Negative relationship with supervisor
3. Policies that do not apply to everyone equally	3. Elimination of employee's job responsibilities in areas affected by those policies
4. Innovative ideas that would change the status quo	4. Stereotyping of employee's personality and perhaps even of employee's spirituality
5. Christian principles that apply to those the organization serves but not to the organization itself	5. Loss of job

One of the most vivid accounts of repercussions I have encountered appeared in an article in the *Chicago Tribune* several years ago. It describes a theology professor's personal conflict with the school's administration:

Because of the nature of my courses, the subject of feminism and equality in the church didn't come up very often, but ocasionally [sic] it would and I'd always be careful to present both sides of the issue. I tried to be balanced. I didn't ride the issue as a hobby horse. But the students all knew how I felt about it; I think most of the faculty did.

I assumed the administration did as well because when the new dean of faculty came in three years ago . . . , I was concerned that I level with him, so I told him what my views on the subject were. I added that my wife had a book coming out on the subject that was sure to raise some questions, and I just wanted him to know where I stood.

He assured me there was no problem, and even added that he had some sympathy for the position himself. So I never hid anything under the rug. I was very, very clear. . . .

[Soon afterward, however, this respected and popular professor of theology] was told he could not address the issue of feminism again in the classroom because a summer student of his had complained about [his] position—a position, the administration claimed, that conflicted with [the school's].

"As far as I knew, the school had no formal position. . . . There is nothing in the doctrine statements we sign each year which even touches on the subject. They said the fact that women could not take the pastors major was evidence of their position, but that didn't make sense to me; it was inconsistent. For instance, women can take the missions major and go out in some other country and perform the work of a missionary, which is basically the work of the pastor in this country. Or they can take the Bible theology major, which most students consider to be better preparation for becoming a pastor than [the] pastors major.

Furthermore, in our evening school, women who are pastors in the black community can come and take our courses and they're already ordained."

[The professor] sumbitted [sic] a letter of protest to the [administration], in which he argued that feminism "was a matter about which there ought to be freedom of conscience among faculty members." [The dean of the faculty] responded with the promise of a "careful, detailed, and prompt reply."

The reply came on Aug. 1 with [the dean's] request for [the professor's] resignation . . . . Officers of the school have refused comment on the controversy . . . .

[The professor concluded by saying:] *"The school should be open for discussion and differences of opinion. My . . . concern is the fact that what happened to me could happen to anyone at [that school]—all of it behind your back with no chance for a grievance procedure"* [emphasis mine].[5]

My reason for including this rather lengthy account is not in any way to disparage the Christian institution involved or its officials. Nor am I interested in making a hero out of the professor involved. What I do want to show is an example of the reality of repercussions in Christian institutions. Here is one situation where discussion and differences of opinion were tightly controlled, where things that were important to one's well-being were decided behind one's back, and where there was "no chance for a grievance procedure." One man spoke out, tried to discuss the undiscussable, and got the ax.

However, that is only one of the possible repercussions. The possibilities range from humiliation, peer rejection and poor relationships with superiors to reduction in pay, demotion and, as in the professor's case, being fired. Nevertheless, one stands out above all the rest. The single most feared repercussion is *loss of credibility*.[6]

Loss of credibility occurs when one is seen as a troublemaker or a poor team player. Quite often the person involved is labeled as having an attitude problem or as insubordinate. However, most of the time these labels seem to be a result more of wanting to maintain control than actual flaws in the person who has lost credibility.

Unfortunately, regardless of the truth of the label, the label will have an effect. Once a person has been labeled a troublemaker, it sets in motion an incremental repercussion process that workers everywhere have come to dread. The first repercussion is a loss of influence and opportunities to contribute on important matters. The "troublemaker" is excluded from information loops—he or she is simply no longer seen as an important contributor.

The effects of labeling also reach deeply into a person. The next level of repercussions follows rather closely to what you read about Larry earlier. One of the first changes in a person who loses credibility is the withdrawing of allegiance to the organization.

This is followed by a drop in productivity and work quality. Finally, a self-critical attitude develops, resulting in any number of negative emotions. They can range from hurt, anger and depression to feeling unfit, unworthy and unwanted.

Control

What produces the climate of fear that leads to such devastating results? I have come to the conclusion that control is the dynamic behind fear of repercussions and the resulting havoc in people's lives. Control is the driving force that keeps people from speaking up, for fear that something bad will happen if they do. Control tells them the way things are going to be and insists that any other alternatives are wrong.

Control does not operate in a vacuum. It needs effort—lots of it. People who want to control others must work at it. And they do. The tools they use are called *control devices,* that are set up to manipulate people and keep them in line. Here are a few:

1. **The *loyalty* control device**—requiring personal sacrifice as a sign of commitment to the team, and dispensing favors or giving recognition to those who respond favorably in order to instill a sense of loyalty to oneself or to the organization. This can be very powerful, and it can be used very inappropriately.

For example, consider the supervisor who puts pressure on workers to regularly work overtime, and then who looks favorably on them when they record only the time worked during normal working hours. (We will look at the personal and interpersonal dynamics involved, but we will leave aside the legal issues that also are involved.) For those workers who have a strong sense of integrity, such a set of expectations violates their moral code. It also forces them to choose between spending all their time and energy at an unhealthy work site and having sufficient opportunities for creating healthy relationships outside of work.

For those workers who capitulate, working unusually long hours and lying about it cause a loss of both quality of life and integrity. In addition, the supervisor is given an excuse to promote workers who appear to be committed to the team but who do not otherwise deserve a promotion. The double deception of lying and promoting creates and motivates at least the appearance of loyalty, which the supervisor will use for even more manipulation in the future. The workers who have capitulated and who have been promoted by deception will be expected to conform without complaint—until they do not have a life of their own. And the workers who have maintained their integrity and who have not been promoted will have to put up with cutting comments like this: "If they can do it, so can you!"

2. The *fair-haired boy* control device—making comments to you that discredit others in the organization but make you feel like you have an "in." This also builds loyalty and makes it hard to go against the grain.

3. The *blind-trust* control device—demanding blind trust, backed by subtle threats linked to job security. This exerts pressure to go along and to be a good team member, with the implication that only good team members will survive.

4. The *unanimity* control device—making people feel that any form of dispute regarding how the organization is run is destructive. The emphasis is again on teamwork, with an added emphasis on compliance with the norm. The message is basically that there must be perfect harmony (or at least the appearance of it).

5. The *gatekeeper* control device—allowing only supervisory personnel or management to communicate to the next level of the administrative hierarchy. So, when there is a complaint at the bottom, it is subject to all sorts of self-serving changes on its way to the top. This is a favorite device of anxious managers and of insecure pastors who do not want to be truly accountable to their boards.

6. The *gelding* control device—withholding complete information so that people who complain can be made to feel like fools; they can simply be told that they do not have all the facts. In C. S. Lewis's words, those who use this control device "castrate and bid the geldings be fruitful."[7]

7. The *sacrificial lamb* control device—dividing and conquering: "If you have a complaint, come to me with it and do

not mention it to anyone else." Such an order removes any possibility of joining forces for mutual support and encouragement and instead produces isolation and intimidation. People who are fired are often told this, since it removes the possibility of open dialogue and exposure of injustices.

This listing of control devices is by no means an exhaustive list, nor is it based on a scientific procedure for data collection. I have simply collected a number of impressions through the years that I think are pretty accurate. I've "been there" with every one of these control devices. I know the resentment that the loyalty control device builds in those who are forced to choose between promotion and integrity. I have been a fair-haired boy, and it has made me feel very uncomfortable, not only from being drawn into the sin of gossip but also from realizing that I could be the one who is discredited next. I have seen the blind-trust control device make a lot of people very angry, since they are exhorted to simply trust the leadership, without any supporting evidence as to why they should.

I also have felt the superficial peace-at-any-cost of the unanimity control device, which is often seen in Christian organizations, and I have seen the resultant stifling of the Spirit in those with discernment. I know the agony of Christian organizations killing themselves from the inside because of the information control involved in the gatekeeper control device. And I have shared the powerlessness of many a gelding and sacrificial lamb, who have come to me in tears after being closeted in the office of a Christian boss and then verbally brutalized.

Control is like a cancer: It grows until it is cut out or kills. Control ultimately corrupts the entire system. In the end, we only want to serve those who are above us, control those who are below us and compete with those who are our peers. Serve up. Control down. Compete across.

Many of us know what a control-dominated organization does to people. But let me make it more explicit. It turns us into *drones* and *eunuchs*. That's right, organizational drones[8] and organizational eunuchs.[9] (I apologize to my female readers for these phrases.)

Consider the organization where the well-being of everyone depends on the vision and inspiration of a single individual within the organization. This single individual is a sort of hero, and everyone else is a drone, with little opportunity to use judgment or take initiative. Organizational drones do not speak out and are not creative. They are only pliable and reliable.

Pastors sometimes mistakenly play the part of the "hero"; they try to control all the ministries within their church. They do not equip others to start new ministries and take responsibility for them. These pastors often feel threatened if they can't control all aspects of the work within their church. Everyone else is just a drone.

Now consider the organization where unanimity is so highly valued that it carries more weight with individuals than do their own consciences, and where the appearance of harmony is maintained by manipulating words to create false realities. For individuals working in that kind of organization, agreeableness and politeness take on a much higher value than accountability and truthfulness. These people become organizational eunuchs.

Have I described your experience? Is your place of work or worship built around a single individual, a hero, who is defining past, present and future realities for you? Are these realities based predominantly on this leader's own subjective, impressionistic data about how things are, rather than on more objective data? Is God-talk or spiritual jargon that bolsters the leader's view of reality used to propagandize internally and posture the organization externally?

Does the leader ask for real opinions and questions? Or is everything supposed to be exciting and enjoyable, and every question supposed to be a phony question, where the answer is already known by everyone and is then rehearsed to demonstrate consensus? Are the unpleasant realities of your organization's "Babylon" being shut out, and the Lord's songs being sung as if His kingdom were already here—right here in your organization? Do you know what's really going on and, therefore, refuse to sing along? Consider the lament of the Psalmist, who felt the same way: "Weeping, we sat beside the rivers of Babylon thinking of Jerusalem. We have put away our lyres, hanging them upon the branches of the willow trees, for how can we sing? Yet our captors, our tormentors, demand that we sing for them the happy songs of Zion!"[10]

Whatever your wounds, whatever reasons you have for not speaking up, whatever control devices are being used to keep you in line, whatever songs you as a weeping, wounded warrior will not sing—remember: You are not alone. Hear the words of a well-known author, who suffered unbearable pain from the way other Christian leaders treated her, and who agonized over the way Christian publishers made her feel utterly untouchable after her widely publicized divorce. Without judging the rightness or wrongness of her situation, let her words speak to your heart:

> We all wait together, trying to make sense out of our ordeal, trying to cope with the crisis of the moment, trying to persevere in spite of the shattering brokenness of our experience, trying to find some meaning in our suffering, and trying somehow to find our way back into wholeness and hope once more.[11]

In our woundedness, we all wait together. Let us now begin the journey toward recovery together.

2

GUIDELINES

FOR RECOVERY

I BELIEVE THERE IS A BIBLICAL PATTERN FOR RECOVERY. It is a pattern of recognition, remembrance and response, and it is found in both the Old and New Testament.

Consider, for example, the Old Testament story of Joseph's recovery from his jealous older brothers' plotting to kill him and selling him into Egypt. Joseph was only seventeen when the story began with his brothers' acts of treachery. We know from the account in Genesis that he cried out to his brothers, pleading for his life from the empty well where they had violently thrown him. But his anguished sobs fell upon deaf ears. For twenty-two years this scene smoldered in all of their consciences, eventually burning its way into their very souls.

Think about Joseph after he got out of that well—on the long, filthy, dangerous trip to Egypt in the slave caravan. What was he thinking about? I would guess his heart ached from the undeserved cruelty shown toward him by his brothers. He must have felt more like an object than a person, an object that was to be sold to the highest bidder. To make matters worse, he had to know that he was helpless to do anything about it.

Had Joseph lost all hope for the future? Did he give up on God's great purpose for him, which had been implied through the dreams he had earlier? All we know for sure is that the implications of power and prosperity in Joseph's dreams did in fact become reality once he got to Egypt. Through the years, God blessed him mightily: Joseph first prospered in the house of Potiphar, then was given unprecedented power in the land of Pharaoh. "The Lord was with Joseph."[1] That, too, was burned into Joseph's soul.

Fast-forward to the seven-year worldwide famine, during which time "Joseph was in control of the land, in charge of sales [of grain] to all the people of the earth."[2] So Joseph's brothers came to Egypt in search of grain and found themselves in Joseph's presence. They, of course, did not recognize him, but he recognized them. Here they were, in flesh and blood, the brothers who had abused him so wickedly so long ago. Joseph had taken the first step of biblical recovery: *recognition.*

After a period of putting his brothers to the test, to see if they had changed for the better, Joseph finally disclosed his true identity. He also told his brothers not to be distressed and angry at themselves for selling him into Egypt. He remembered that God sent him ahead of them to save their lives. "It was not you who sent me here, but God."[3] Joseph had taken the second step: *remembrance.*

Joseph then took the third step: *response.* He arranged for the entire family of seventy to settle in the best of the land, the land of Goshen. And, seventeen years later, when his soul-sick brothers pleaded with him to forgive their sins against him, Joseph responded again with reassurance and kindness. He told them not to be afraid, that vengeance was the Lord's, and that although they had planned evil against him, the Lord intended it for good. "So then, don't be afraid. I will provide for you and your children."[4]

Just before he died, Joseph responded a third time, "I am about to die. But God will surely come to your aid and take you up out of this land to the land he promised on oath to Abraham, Isaac and Jacob."[5] What a wonderful benediction and expression of hope for their future. Clearly, Joseph's recovery was complete.

The biblical account of Jesus in the Garden of Gethsemane dramatically compresses the process but reveals the same pattern demonstrated by Joseph surviving in Egypt and sending his family to the land of Goshen. Jesus and His disciples had just eaten their last meal together, and they talked about the fact that one of them would betray Jesus and another would disown Him. As they came to the Garden, Jesus began to feel deeply alarmed and distressed. He *recognized* that His soul was mortally grieved. He *remembered*, however, that "Father, all things are possible with Thee!" That led to two conflicting statements: "Remove this cup from Me!" and, "Not, however, what I will; but what Thou wilt!"[6]

I would like to reflect for a moment on the matter of the cup.[7] The communion cup that the disciples drank from at the Last Supper and that we drink from at the Lord's Supper is referred to in Luke's Gospel as "the cup after supper."[8] Paul calls it "the cup of blessing."[9] I find it interesting that in the Haggadah, the Jewish Passover liturgy, the third cup—the cup after supper—is given the same name, the Cup of Blessing.

In the Haggadah, there is also a fourth cup, which is called the Cup of Acceptance. The significance of this cup is that it recalls to us the tasks that still await us. Jesus drank the third cup of the Passover that night in the upper room, and then he told the disciples, "I will not drink again of the fruit of the vine until that day when I drink it anew in the kingdom of God."[10] Could it be that Jesus did not drink the fourth cup because of the disturbance in His soul about how it applied to Himself?

Since Jesus was both God and man, His human will did not always conform without a struggle to His divine will. Therefore it is understandable that He would initially want this Cup of Acceptance—of His death and all that it implied—removed from Him. Ultimately, He *responded*, not with resignation but with resolve, "Not, however, what I will; but what Thou wilt!" This response revealed that, metaphorically speaking, Jesus had in fact drunk the Cup of Acceptance.

As you face unpleasant and seemingly unbearable tasks that lie ahead in your recovery process, you will benefit greatly by relating the example of Jesus and the two cups to your situation. First, it is absolutely essential that you remember your identity—who you are—in the Lord, and that with Him, all things are possible. This is your Cup of Blessing. You must drink your Cup of Blessing. Then, you must resolve to trust God while facing the hard tasks that lie ahead. This will give you peace in your soul as you continue to respond in accordance with who God is and in agreement with His will, not your own. This is your Cup of Acceptance. You must drink your Cup of Acceptance.

THREE PHASES OF RECOVERY

As we looked at the biblical accounts of Joseph and Jesus, a pattern emerged: recognition, remembrance and response. We can now apply this pattern to the description of a three-phase process to help Christian workers recover from their woundedness.

Phase One of the recovery process is *recognizing* the situation for what it really is. What are you up against? Is the organization itself sick or abusive in some way? Is the problem entirely with someone else, or, on the other hand, do you add something to it also? What do you personally bring to the party psychologically and spiritually that makes you vulnerable to abuse, and that therefore makes matters worse for you?

Phase Two is *remembering* what the situation ideally should be. It is moving in your mind from what is to what should be, with biblical reality checks of the three main components of your situation: the organization, the leadership and yourself. Phase Two is the pause in the process that first, grounds you in who you are as defined by God, not your situation, and second, gives you the perspective of God's thoughts of what your organization and its leadership should be. Remembering your Christian identity and your Christian ideals is *drinking the Cup of Blessing*, which blesses the entire recovery process.

Let's revisit the lament of the captives by the rivers of Babylon, this time using the Amplified Version of the Bible:

> By the rivers of Babylon, there we (captives) sat down, yes, we wept when we (earnestly) remembered Zion (city of our God imprinted on our hearts).

On the willow trees in the midst of (Babylon) we hung our harps.

For there they who led us captive required of us a song with words; and our tormentors *and* they who wasted us required of us mirth, saying, Sing us one of the songs of Zion.

How shall we sing the Lord's song in a strange land?[11]

These people remembered God's thoughts for them and persevered, keeping their identity in the midst of torment. They were captives in a strange land, but they remembered Zion and refused to be compromised. You, too, must have God's thoughts for you imprinted on your heart. You, too, must remain true to your calling in the midst of torment. By refusing to compromise your trust in God, you are *drinking the Cup of Acceptance,* which prepares you for the hard tasks that lie ahead.

Phase Three is *responding* to your situation by choosing whether to seek relief within the situation or to seek release from the situation. You must either work to make the situation better, or leave—unless, of course, you have already been let go. In the latter case, only the first two phases will apply to your recovery: recognizing accurately and honestly what really happened, and remembering your calling as a Christian so that you don't get drawn into acting like your tormentors.

There are three choices for responding. First, you may choose to *minister to others* while abiding in your suffering. I do not mean withdrawing and wallowing in your pain. I mean being an intentional witness for Christ in your daily walk, or coming alongside others in their suffering, as a wounded healer. Second, you may choose to attempt to *make changes*, hoping to help move the organization closer to the ideal of what an organization ought to be like. But, if you do, you must know who the real enemy is and be willing to engage in spiritual warfare. Third, you may choose to *move on.* If you do, you must know whether it is within God's will, and you must leave in a God-honoring way.

In summary:

THE THREE PHASES OF RECOVERY
- Recognizing—what is
- Remembering—what should be
- Responding—what can be done about it

Anticipatory Anxiety

Satan tries to prevent recovery. One of the tools he uses is fear, which prevents you from responding to your situation and completing your recovery. It is a self-perpetuating cycle of fear that keeps you locked in your woundedness. Have you experienced the fear that keeps you paralyzed in your pain, powerless and without hope, even though you know exactly what you are up against, and you are remaining faithfully true to your identity as a Christian? Have you experienced the fear that, while you bring the Cup of Blessing to your lips to drink, breaks the Cup of Acceptance under your feet?

This paralyzing fear is called *anticipatory anxiety*. It is a general state of anticipation that something bad is going to happen or that something good is not going to happen. It is a pervasive apprehensiveness, ranging from fear of repercussions to fear that nothing will change.

We can refer to the self-perpetuating cycle of fear as the *anticipatory anxiety cycle*. Here is how it works. Note again the three choices for responding under Phase Three: minister to others, make changes or move on. When we think about these choices, we think about the following:

MINISTERING TO OTHERS	MAKING CHANGES	MOVING ON
• Carrying the freight	• Fighting for change	• Taking flight
• Carrying the weight of others' suffering	• Making things right	• Picking up our marbles and going home

But when we think about making one of the three choices, we also think about the downside: It is frightening. And the more we think, the more frightened we get. This all works out as depicted on the following cycle. Start anywhere on the cycle and move around it clockwise.

Think about *fight*: "I just have to speak up. This place uses and abuses people, then spits them out and throws them away."

Which causes *fright*: "If I speak up, I'll get canned. Or, they'll just ignore me, and nothing will change."

Which leads to thoughts of *flight*: "But I can't keep putting up with this garbage. I am not going to take it any more. I have to find some other place where I won't be abused and be made to feel so useless."

Which cause more *fright*: "No, I can't leave. I'm scared. What would happen if I don't find a better place?"

Which leads to thoughts of *carrying the freight*: "If I stay, maybe I can be used by God to help others. Everybody's hurting. Maybe my understanding can give others hope."

Which cause more *fright*: "If I stay, I'll be totally wasted. I won't be any good to anybody."

Which leads again to thoughts of *fight*: " But I'm going to stand up for what I believe. God will honor me if I take a stand."

And around and around we go—again and again.

Draw your own anticipatory anxiety cycle, and write in the words you would use to describe your experience as you go around the cycle. What are your thoughts and feelings as you reflect on your situation?

The anticipatory anxiety cycle is a self-reinforcing cycle that perpetuates itself and can be stopped only when thought is translated into action. You can break the cycle only by committing yourself to helping change things for the better, by leaving, or by intentionally witnessing for Christ or coming alongside other wounded workers as a wounded healer.

BIBLICAL GUIDELINES FOR THE RESPONSE PHASE

I have known Christian workers who, while abiding in their suffering, spent all of their energy pleading with God to make things better only for themselves. Their focus did not include helping others with their suffering but was exclusively on relieving themselves of their own suffering.

I have known Christian workers who felt it was time to move on but who were contemplating leaving for the wrong reason. For example, they denied their own responsibility in dealing with their problems. Instead, they blamed their woes entirely on their boss for rejecting them, their coworkers for impeding their spiritual growth, or the organization for imagined misdeeds that simply were not true. By refusing to work on their own issues, they missed the opportunity to improve their situation.

I have known Christian workers who worked for change but didn't seem to get very far. In fact, they actually made matters worse. They fought fire with fire, as if to say, "I am in the right, and I am going to win." Their actions and attitude, however, led them nowhere but further away from a peaceful solution.

To avoid making the mistakes I have just mentioned, you will need biblical guidelines for responding. Whether you choose to ride it out, to run, or to fight for what is right, you need to look no further than to the cross on which Jesus was crucified.

Biblical Guideline One

Picture Christ on the cross, between two thieves.[12] Listen to the first thief utter, sneeringly, "Aren't you the Christ? Save yourself and us!" The biblical account indicates that this man was quite likely full of bitterness and contempt. The only god he understood would act in power to give him what he wanted, when he wanted it. "Why should I put up with this?" he might have been asking himself. "Jesus doesn't have any power. What a poor excuse for a Messiah."

The second thief, however, reproved the first, pointing out that they were suffering justly, while Jesus was not. He then said, "Jesus, remember me when you come into your kingdom." He asked and in *faith* believed his request would not be denied.[13]

In many ways, people who have been victimized in an organizational setting are like that first thief. They are bitter about their circumstances, and they blame God for not making things better. Or perhaps they blame their boss or their pastor. Or maybe they prefer to beg. They implore, they beseech, and they may even formally petition their boss or pastor to relieve them of their pain. Their most forceful petitions, however, are to God, to manipulate Him to rescue them. Surely, they assume, He will remove their pain.

When begging fails, perhaps they take matters into their own hands and attempt to right the wrongs themselves. But then they may become thieves again—looters and plunderers of material and human resources, wrongfully using supplies and services and recruiting followers for their self-serving cause. The response from the powers-that-be is totally predictable: They start condemning and shaming. On top of everything else, now the victims must deal with blame and shame. As beggars, they are discouraged and disheartened. As thieves, they are disgraced.

Looking back at that second thief, it is noteworthy that he simply said to Jesus, "*Remember me* when you come into your kingdom." He did not demand, like the first thief, "Aren't you the Christ? *Save me!*" His interest was in God Himself, not in getting God to change his circumstance. To him, God was not a God of personal circumstances, nor should God be that for us.

Many of us will say right away that change of our circumstance is precisely what we want, and that we want it more than anything else. I understand. But the thief on the cross instructs us to look to God Himself first. Do not look to change first. This is consistent with what God said to Moses at the burning bush.[14] Moses, I am sure, would have preferred the golden scepter of a king to really make things happen. But God simply asked Moses, "What is in your hand?" A plain old staff was in his hand, and that is what God used. God may or may not *change* our circumstance, but He will *use* what is in our hand—our circumstance—for His glory.

The lesson from the cross and the staff is biblical guideline one: Ask in faith for God to remember you—do not demand that God change your circumstance.

Biblical Guideline Two

It will be helpful for you to now consider what you bring to the cross. Are you bitter over what has happened to you, blaming—with good cause—the one who has done you wrong? Have you tried to make things right on your own and unfortunately ended up doing wrong, as well as being wronged? Are blame and shame making your wound even deeper? Is disgrace all you can expect from this?

Are you begging the leadership of the organization to set things right and relieve you of your unbearable pain, knowing that you cannot bear the burden alone and that you cannot just sit back and let the situation continue? Are you discouraged and disheartened? Is your pleading only resulting in disrespect from those who should be supporting you? Do you just want to run?

Are you willing to acknowledge the *truth* of your circumstance, in all of its aspects? Or are you refusing to acknowledge the truth as you come to the foot of the cross? For example, are you denying that you have gained nothing but dishonor and disrespect from your blaming and begging of others? And, do you accept the fact that you may have done additional things that have only deepened your wound?

Or are you perhaps denying the seriousness of the offense toward you, denying that it ever happened, or diminishing its consequences? "That wasn't really a lie. It was just his perception." "I guess he didn't actually say that. He said he didn't." "Sure it was the wrong thing to do, but he's the president, and he can do what he wants."

Sometimes you may get help from others in not acknowledging the truth. They want you to spiritualize it away. They want you to accept the situation as it is, without acknowledging that the consequences of it are bad and that something must be done. They tell you not to challenge authority, that God has set leaders over you whom you must obey. Or, finally, they will say, "Yes, you have been wronged, but you must just give it to God and forget about it, and He will bless you anyway."

By denying the truth of your circumstance, you deny personal responsibility, and you forfeit the opportunity for personal growth as well as improvement of your situation. In addition, you may leave for the wrong reason. This is biblical guideline two: Acknowledge the truth of your circumstance—do not deny your blaming or begging of others and your getting dishonor and disrespect in return; and do not deny the seriousness of your circumstance or try to spiritualize it away.

Biblical Guideline Three

Faith is the bottom line of guideline one, and truth is the bottom line of guideline two. Faith and truth are what you must bring to the cross—to the foot of the cross upon which Jesus was crucified. But what do you find when you get there? Right away you hear Jesus cry out, "My God, my God, why have you forsaken me?"[15] Forsaken—that's what you feel. Does Jesus really know what it is like to be abandoned, like you have at work or at church? You then realize that yes, He does. He was alone in Gethsemane, praying while others slept. He was alone before Caiaphus, and outside the closed doors Peter was denying Him. He was alone before Herod and Pilate. And He was alone in the hands of the soldiers, who stripped, mocked and beat him. He was alone when the crowd chanted, "Crucify him, crucify him, crucify him!"

Have you prayed for human decency to return to your place of work while others slept? Have you, too, been on trial—called on the carpet for speaking up—while those who agreed with you in private now deny you? Have you spoken the truth to your boss and been given a deaf ear? Have you been stripped of your dignity and worth because your church treats women as second-class citizens? Do you feel beaten and crucified by the organized church because they will not accept your giftedness?

Up to this point it may seem pretty even, as far as who was lonelier: Jesus or you. It was Jesus, however, on the cross, not you. *He* was on the cross for *you*.

Oh, how forsaken He must have felt on the cross—the pain, the weakening from loss of blood, the full impact of His lonely destiny of suffering so that others might live. All the while, He was misunderstood and rejected. Reduced to agony, stretched out and hanging from that filthy cross, His heart must have cried out for some word of heavenly comfort, some confirmation of God's presence, some indication that things would somehow be different.

Jesus died. God did not change His circumstance. So, is that it for us then? Is that the message of the cross: We die, and God does not intervene? No, we must go much deeper than that, to the fact that God did intervene by putting Christ on the cross in the first place. It was not just our sin that put Christ on the cross. It was also God's loving provision of His only Son to suffer and die for us. Jesus showed us the way, the way of the cross, and that way is *love*. Jesus showed us that God does not fall back on power or might to defeat sin, but that God instead works through love.

Are you fighting for what is right, and everything is turning out wrong? And if so, have you decided to fight fire with fire? The deeper reality of the cross is biblical guideline three: Act in love—do not defeat with might in order to make things right.

In summary:

Biblical Guidelines for Responding

	Do	Don't
• **Faith**	Ask in faith for God to remember you	Demand that God change your circumstance
• **Truth**	Acknowledge the truth of your circumstance	Deny your blaming or begging of others and your

Do		*Don't*
		getting dishonor and disrespect in return
		Deny the seriousness of your circumstance or try to spiritualize it away
• **Love**	Act in Love	Defeat with might in order to make things right

Recovery is completed—always—by *asking* in faith for God to remember you, by *acknowledging* the truth of your circumstance, and by *acting* in love. Whatever you do, you must act in love.

PHASE ONE

RECOGNIZING

Uncovering the Neurotic Organization

CHARISMATIC LEADERS LOVE TO BE ON CENTER STAGE. They love to draw attention to themselves. They are charming, warm and generous. Their flip side, however, is their superficiality and the manipulation and control that they exert over those who feed on freely given attention and praise.

I have noticed that charismatic leaders almost always have a shadow side, or dark side. A friend of mine, Steve, worked on the administrative team of a Christian institution with a charismatic president. All the members of the team, except Steve, were subservient and compliant—always eager to do whatever the president wanted. Steve began questioning some of the president's impulsive, unchallenged decisions and mentioned that the board ought to know what was going on as a result of some of those decisions. The president was enraged at Steve and met with him in private to tell him so. It was a three-hour tirade from the president of verbal abuse, threats, yelling, swearing and condemnation. Steve was nauseated and humiliated. He was truly a sacrificial lamb.

In sum, this president drew attention to himself and drew others to himself. He would show off in public and be compassionate in private. His warmth and generosity, however, were self-serving. Both praise and lack of praise were used as a control device. He picked subordinates who would be his friends—who would agree with him and not challenge his impulsive decisions. Criticism was seen as insubordination, and all communication was tightly controlled. When he felt threatened, he could abuse as easily as he could charm. His friendships did not run deep.

Such presidents, in effect, define the organization they lead. They do more than correct this and change that. They do more than refocus the vision and mission, rebuild the infrastructure, and restructure the financial base. They redefine the personality of the entire organization. More specifically, *their personality* redefines the personality of the organization. This is not at all unusual in Christian organizations—even those that claim to be founded on biblical principles and to be focused on being *Christ-centered* in all that they do. It is more than a little disconcerting how frequently these organizations seem to be totally dominated by the human personality at the top.

CHARACTERISTICS OF NEUROTIC ORGANIZATIONS

Researchers are finding valid connections between the health of the personalities of corporate executives and the health of their organizations. Leaders, like everyone else, are driven by aspirations, fears and fantasies. These forces in a leader's personality can be very powerful, and when they are neurotic, chances are the organization will be so as well.

What does it mean to be *neurotic*? It means to exhibit behavior that can be described in any number of ways—grandiose, insincere, inconsiderate, impulsive, compulsive, dogmatic, intolerant of ambiguity, suspicious, irrational, depressed, indecisive or withdrawn. It is a self-serving denial or distortion of God-given reality. In a way, everyone is neurotic—perhaps depressed occasionally, irrational at times, suspicious once in awhile, and so on. We all are some of these things at times. But when these behaviors begin to increase in frequency and duration, we become more inflexible and cannot adjust very well to changing situations. We are not crazy, but we are less effective, and we frequently act inappropriately. Our neurotic behavior directly affects the quality of our performance, and it indirectly affects the quality of life of those around us. If we are in a key leadership capacity, the entire organization can become neurotic as a result.

Scientific study of organizational pathology has identified five common types of neurotic organizations: dramatic, compulsive, suspicious, depressive and detached. We will next examine the characteristics of the leader, the organization and the workers that are frequently found in these types of neurotic organizations.[1]

The Leader

Leaders of neurotic organizations are often charismatic, much like the one described at the beginning of this chapter. These leaders are not charismatic in the theological sense. Rather, they are good at generating widespread loyalty and enthusiasm. They may have grandiose thoughts and may want to impress important people and receive appreciation from them. They crave constant stimulation, activity, visibility and excitement. However, in the midst of their flurry of activities, these leaders often lack self-discipline. They just want to "get on with it." The result is sporadic and often misguided innovations, without the formation of the organizational structures needed to back them up.

These leaders have a high need to be nourished by others through confirming and admiring responses. However, though they themselves can be charming, warm and generous, they can also be insincere and inconsiderate and even exploitative. They can also be downright vindictive, letting loose pent-up feelings of rage as they overreact to a challenge to their power. They seem to fluctuate back and forth, over-idealizing some thing or person one moment and devaluing the same thing or person the next.

Leaders of neurotic organizations are often compulsively control oriented. They like to run everything, and to know what is going on at every level of the organization. Some may be excessively concerned about order and efficiency, and preoccupied with trivial details and rules. They may also crave certainty, with no surprises, and may be quite dogmatic and intolerant of ambiguity.

Neurotic leaders may be hypersensitive to hidden motives and to being kept out of the information loop. The intentions of others are misread and perhaps even distorted to fit with unsubstantiated suspicions. When these leaders suspect disobedient behavior or a defiant attitude, they let it add up in their own minds. Finally, given an opportunity, they take it out on the individual. They can be very spiteful.

In the worst-case scenario, leaders of neurotic organizations become hopeless and helpless themselves. They become pessimistic, indecisive and even reclusive. They feel inadequate and believe that they do not have what it takes to revitalize the organization. In fact, they usually begin to look to someone else. If it's a Christian organization, they often look to a big name in the Christian world who has a successful program or idea that can be copied. They hope that imitating it will bale them out and help them avoid facing up to a difficult situation.

They withdraw from the activities around them and make decisions behind closed doors. They rely on reports in the decision-making process rather than on relationships. These leaders daydream about other areas of interest to compensate for their lack of fulfillment at work. They are not interested in people. They are emotionally cool and aloof and are unaffected by the feelings of others. They are also unaffected by praise or criticism. They care little about what others have to say about them.

The Organization

The leadership style that frequently permeates and is passed down through the neurotic organization is impulsive and impressionistic. In other words, decisions are made with very little reflection or analysis, and are based on hunches, not facts. Leaders at all levels tend to overreact to minor events, and also tend to meddle even in routine matters, so that they can put their own stamp on them and take credit if credit is due.

The leadership style may, in many cases, be extremely hierarchical, with an excessive reliance on rigid formal codes and elaborate information systems in order to maintain internal control. Sometimes the rules are legacies of the past, which are really due to nothing more than an obsession with the founding fathers' ideas. This creates tunnel vision and an inability to adapt to new ideas. Form takes precedence over substance. Sometimes the routine becomes so well established, with a mature constituency and time-tested programs that have been run the same way for years, that leaders at every level of the organization are merely caretakers who live in the past.

In some cases the leadership style throughout the neurotic organization has a calculating and continual watchfulness that tries to identify potential external enemies—people and organizations to blame for something. For example, a Christian organization might have no Christian distinctiveness to push—just a perpetual vigilance against "bad guys" to punish. Such vigilance can also be directed internally and is usually politically motivated. Groups jostle for power, and individuals jockey for position. All gain is at someone else's expense.

The *culture* of neurotic organizations is frequently venturesome, daring, and even arrogant, and strives for unbridled growth. This type of culture can also encourage a worshipful attitude toward the leader and an unquestioning climate of subordination, where communication is mostly top-down, and dissent and criticism of the leadership are not tolerated.

In contrast, the culture may be bureaucratic, where the climate is still oriented toward control, but where the mindset is oriented toward caution. This culture is inwardly focused on rules and regulations—but for indoctrination, not for empowerment of the workers. The bureaucratic mentality of this culture has four parts:[2]

1. *Patriarchal atmosphere*. The organization is defined by its traditional, hierarchical, high-control orientation.
2. *Self-interest*. Success is defined as being financially rewarded for moving up the ladder, as opposed to being engaged in meaningful work.
3. *Manipulative tactics*. The patriarchal atmosphere and personal ambition conspire to support behavior that is calculated, cautious and circuitous.

4. *Dependency*. The first three parts combine to create the fourth part: the belief that one's survival is determined by being willing to do whatever it takes to get ahead (even suspending one's Christian values), while relying on the support of a hierarchical, power-oriented organizational culture.

The organizational culture may be cautious to the extreme. It may be paranoid—having an atmosphere where guardedness, distrust and suspicion are pervasive. This kind of corporate paranoia often has its beginnings during a significant challenge to the organization's core values or existence. Perhaps the senior pastor of a church has been found to be involved in an adulterous relationship. Or perhaps a new church has been established nearby and is drawing members away. Whatever it may be, an alarm sounds loudly and clearly. Every member must be closely monitored for moral failure or for flagging motivation regarding membership. Everyone must be under continuous surveillance.

The organizational culture may also have a mentality that is bureaucratic to the extreme. It may be highly politicized—having an atmosphere of personal ambition, greed, and self-centeredness. An organization with this type of neurotic culture is most likely just a collection of independent and alienated fiefdoms. The climate is one of political infighting—everyone either lobbies for or conspires against the leader for personal gain. It can become a conspiratorial free-for-all.

The Workers
People who work in a neurotic organization sometimes idealize a charismatic leader so much that they will lose their motivation and even their sense of personal worth when he or she leaves. Their worth is all tied up in their perception of being personally connected to the leader. They are accustomed to ingratiating themselves, ignoring the leader's faults and vying with one another for the leader's attention. They feel overly flattered by a few words of praise and are devastated by even mild reprimands or even an unresponsive look or lapse of courtesy.

Because of their vulnerability to the leader's behavior toward them, the workers are unusually subservient and compliant. This makes them very easy to control and manipulate. Many leaders actually seek out subordinates of this kind. But although the workers may start out feeling wanted, they often end up feeling wounded.

If you work for this type of leader, your woundedness may include feeling envious when the leader shows favoritism to others. It may include feeling guilty when the leader seems to frown while making eye contact from across the room. And it may include feeling used and abused when the leader charms and flatters you for awhile, then suddenly devalues and ignores you as though you no longer exist. This kind of behavior and its effect are described vividly in a letter from a friend of mine, a former employee of a parachurch organization:

> A year or two after I left, I saw the president of the organization. She did not see me and turned away. In fact, she did not visibly recognize me at all. Her nonreaction confirmed that the rejection I was feeling at that moment was not personal but tied to the fact that I was no longer productive for the organization. Therefore, I was "dead." In retrospect, the interactions we had when I worked for her, that I felt had been of a personal and affirming nature, were merely interactions of molding and shaping me to her way of thinking.

Workers may not worship the leader, but they may work for a leader who worships thoroughness and exactness. That may be the main source of their woundedness. Everything seems to revolve around avoiding surprises at all costs. Everything the worker does is thoroughly regulated toward that end. But it's like being in a straitjacket. Initiative is stifled. Freedom of choice and personal responsibility are lost. No one can personally influence anything. There is massive discontent.

The greatest wound in this case is fear. If you work in a neurotic organization such as this, you may be scared to death of making a mistake, and you may be fearful that the ax may fall at any time. You may have become indecisive and insecure. You must simply follow in lockstep, following orders precisely and never disagreeing with anything or anybody. Everyone knows that if you are in tune with the leadership, you'll do fine. But if there is an element of discord, you'd better be prepared to be closely scrutinized, perhaps even to the point of total distraction. You can expect to have a fire lit under you, to have the heat turned up, and to be turned slowly on a skewer.

People who work in a paranoid organizational culture work in an atmosphere where distrust and defensiveness loom everywhere. This automatically breeds insecurity. In an atmosphere where even an off-the-cuff remark can cause repercussions, workers hold back and concentrate on protecting themselves from exploitation, and they feel disenchanted and entrapped. They not only fear what the leadership will do, but they also begin to actually fear what the leadership fears. Everyone fears attack—whether on the corporate values or on the organization's continued existence— and everyone's energy is directed toward identifying an enemy that he or she can blame, and toward avoiding taking responsibility for his or her own actions.

When blame is the game, shame is the wound of the workers. With everyone looking around for someone else to blame, you will sooner or later be blamed for someone else's mistake—and experience shame. With everyone being manipulated into worshiping loyalty, you will sooner or later be made to feel disloyal because of some miscue or another—and experience shame. With leaders treating workers as malingerers and incompetents, you will sooner or later lose self-esteem and just want to run away or hide in some safe corner—and experience shame.

People who work in a highly politicized organizational culture become victims of all of the problems of coordination, communication and cooperation that it produces. People don't work together, so projects often cannot be completed. People don't communicate. They'd rather fight. No one cooperates. Everyone's out for himself or herself.

If you work in a neurotic organization like this, the wound of estrangement may describe fairly accurately what you are going through. You may be alienated from a leader who won't even acknowledge that you said something, much less respond to what you said. And since you would normally rely on your leader's input to give you some direction, you may have lost confidence that this person knows what he or she is doing. So, you grow more and more frustrated and bewildered and not just a little concerned about your future in the organization.

One wound creates another, and perhaps you find yourself aggressively competing with others for anything you can get. You're suspicious and distrustful of them, and they are of you as well. You play games. And you all lose.

Sooner or later, whatever the particulars of the neurotic organization that you are in, your wounds will more than likely include a sense of futility, depression, cynicism and apathy.[3] But it does not end with apathy. Apathy is not an end state but rather a preparatory state for the rage that many wounded workers finally come to feel in a neurotic organization.

Let's look at an example of how rage develops. If you work in an atmosphere where there is an exceptionally high tolerance for ineptitude and failure, where initiative is not required or rewarded, and where all suggestions for change are resisted, you will begin to feel pretty worthless. Everyone, however, must have a sense of worth—it is a basic human need. A sense of worth can be defined as feeling significant or as feeling that you are making a difference. Everyone needs to make a difference, however large or small.

You make a difference by having an impact on others. But when all avenues of expression are cut off, and when you are continuously burdened by feelings of impotence, then rage is the predictable end result. And, when all attempts to assert yourself are denied, then you'll blow up. That will have an impact all right, and it will give you back your feeling of significance. But at what a cost! In Christ, there is another way.

PUTTING YOUR ORGANIZATION TO THE TEST

Phase One of the recovery process is assessing your place of work or worship and your own personality. The goal is to gain an accurate understanding of what you are up against, and whether you are making a bad situation worse.

The following test will help you understand what might be wrong with your place of work or worship.[4] The test will help you gain useful information about neurotic processes that quite possibly have become an integral part of your organization. This is not a scientifically validated test. However, the information from the test and the background information about neurotic organizations that was given in the preceding material will help you do the following:

1. Understand what may not be "normal" and what must be changed in your organization.
2. Appreciate that perhaps "your problem" is not just *your* problem.

Place an X in the *Always, Sometimes,* or *Never* column for each item—whichever applies to you and your organization.

ORGANIZATION TEST: NEUROTIC

	Always	Sometimes	Never
1. Does the leader of your organization strive to be on center stage and to draw attention to him/herself by showing off?	☐	☐	☐
2. Does the leader of your organization crave constant stimulation and exciting activities?	☐	☐	☐
3. Does the leader lack self-discipline—does he/she make impulsive decisions without having adequate physical, financial or human resources to back them up?	☐	☐	☐

	Always	Sometimes	Never
4. Does the leader demonstrate a need to be loved by everybody?	☐	☐	☐
5. Is there a tendency for the leader to store up anger toward someone, and then to act irrationally when that person challenges his/her power?	☐	☐	☐
6. Is there a tendency for the leader to be very flattering toward someone one moment, and to be vindictive the next?	☐	☐	☐
7. Does the leader insist on running everything and knowing everything that is going on?	☐	☐	☐
8. Does the leader have an exaggerated fear of surprises?	☐	☐	☐
9. Is the leader pessimistic and indecisive, and does he/she avoid difficult situations?	☐	☐	☐
10. Has the boss/pastor disengaged from the demands of the job and withdrawn emotionally from the employees/church members?	☐	☐	☐

	Always	Sometimes	Never
11. Are decisions made without analysis of objective data?	☐	☐	☐
12. Is the organizational leadership style rigidly hierarchical, and excessively focused on control?	☐	☐	☐
13. Are leaders at every level of the organization so obsessed with the founder's ideas that they are merely caretakers of the past?	☐	☐	☐
14. Is the leadership obsessed with enemies both inside and outside the organization?	☐	☐	☐
15. Are dissent and criticism of the leadership not tolerated?	☐	☐	☐
16. Does the organization have a bureaucratic mentality— defined by a patriarchal atmosphere; personal ambition; manipulative tactics to get ahead at any cost; and dependence on the support of a hierarchical, power-oriented organizational culture?	☐	☐	☐

	Always	Sometimes	Never
17. Is the organizational culture paranoid, with guardedness, distrust and suspicion being pervasive?	❑	❑	❑
18. Is the organizational culture highly politicized—there are fragmented power centers, and the organization has become a conspiratorial free-for-all?	❑	❑	❑
19. Do employees/church members lose their motivation and sense of personal worth when the boss/pastor leaves?	❑	❑	❑
20. Are workers unusually subservient and compliant?	❑	❑	❑
21. Are workers unusually fearful of making a mistake and fearful that at any time they could be let go? Are they indecisive and insecure?	❑	❑	❑
22. Does everyone in the organization look for an enemy that they can blame—thereby avoiding taking responsibility for their own actions?	❑	❑	❑

	Always	Sometimes	Never
23. Are workers made to feel disloyal because of a mistake that they have made and then subjected to shame?	☐	☐	☐
24. Do workers aggressively compete with one another and fight for turf to such an extent that projects cannot be completed?	☐	☐	☐
25. Do the wounds of the workers include a sense of futility, depression, cynicism and apathy?	☐	☐	☐

If you answered *Always* or *Sometimes* to ten or more of the questions, then you are probably in a neurotic organization. You can now see more clearly why it is an upsetting place for you to work or worship. If that is the case, the next test will give you more information to help you decide what you are going to do about your situation.

PUTTING YOURSELF TO THE TEST

What do you bring to the table? Is it really just the boss's or the pastor's problem? Is it just the lousy organization that is messing you up? Or could you be complicating the problem? What do you personally bring to your organization that interacts with the problems you discovered on the previous test, and that makes matters worse?

The following questions relate your personality to the neurotic organization. Opposite each question place an X in the *Yes* column if it applies to you or in the *No* column if it does not. NOTE: answer each question in terms of how it relates to *your personality in general*, not your present situation.

SELF TEST

		Yes	No
1.	Are you often jealous in your relationships with others?	☐	☐
2.	Are you overly sensitive to criticism or personal attack?	☐	☐
3.	Do you aggressively compete and fight for turf?	☐	☐
4.	Do you fear making mistakes?	☐	☐
5.	Are you suspicious by nature?	☐	☐
6.	Do you find it difficult to trust other people?	☐	☐
7.	Do you come from a shame-based background?	☐	☐
8.	Are you often depressed?	☐	☐
9.	Do you usually feel alienated from authority figures and resent restrictive rules?	☐	☐
10.	Do you have a tendency to doubt your worth—to doubt that you can make a difference and have an impact on others?	☐	☐

Which items on the Self Test have marks in the *Yes* column? Turn back to the Organization Test and note which items have marks in the *Always* or *Sometimes* columns. Stop and think about the possible interactions of the items that you have marked.

For example, let's say that on the Self Test you marked *Yes* to the following item: "Are you overly sensitive to criticism or personal attack?" And on the Organization Test you marked *Always* to these items: "Is there a tendency for the leader to store up anger toward someone, and then to act irrationally when that person challenges his/her power?" "Is there a tendency for the leader to be very flattering toward someone one moment, and to be vindictive the next?" and "Does everyone in the organization look for an enemy that they can blame—thereby avoiding taking responsibility for their own actions?" If so, your situation looks like a bomb waiting to go off, doesn't it? And you're sitting right on top of it.

Or let's say that on the Self Test you marked *Yes* to these items: "Do you aggressively compete and fight for turf?" and "Do you usually feel alienated from authority figures and resent restrictive rules?" What if on the Organization Test you marked *Always* to these items: "Is the organizational leadership style rigidly hierarchical, and excessively focused on control?" "Are dissent and criticism of the leadership not tolerated?" "Does the organization have a bureaucratic mentality—defined by a patriarchal atmosphere; personal ambition; manipulative tactics to get ahead at any cost; and dependence on the support of a hierarchical, power-oriented organizational culture?" "Is the organizational culture highly politicized—there are fragmented power centers, and the organization has become a conspiratorial free-for-all?" and "Do workers aggressively compete with one another, and fight for turf to such an extent that projects cannot be completed?"

If you examine this second example, you will see that when you bring your aggressive, competitive personality into an organizational culture that is power-oriented and highly politicized, you are adding fuel to the fire. In this kind of culture, much energy and time are usually consumed by manipulative, conspiratorial infighting, and getting ahead usually replaces getting things done. In such a place, will you find peace, much less get your work done?

In addition, your alienation from authority and resentment of restrictive rules will run head-on into your organization's rigid hierarchical control orientation. And, when you give voice to your feelings with criticism or dissent, you had better "duck" and be prepared for the worst.

Are your personality characteristics compatible with your situation? Or does what you bring to the situation make it worse? Does the combination of your personality and your organization's weaknesses indicate whether you should try to be an agent of change in your job or church?

For example, what if you found on the Organization Test that your organization has a number of weaknesses, and you also found on the Self Test that you do not have any corresponding personality characteristics that would make your situation worse? Does that really mean that things will not get any worse for you than they already are? Does it necessarily mean that you should stay and work for change? Or would doing that possibly in some way actually make things worse, so that you might just as well leave now?

These are the kind of questions wounded workers should ask. We will take them up in chapters 8–10 when we consider directly the question, "Is this a battle I should fight, or a battlefield I should flee?"

Dysfunctional Personality

Consideration needs to be given to the possibility that you have personality problems that should be dealt with separately from your work or ministry. You may find that you are experiencing dysfunctional emotions, moods, actions and reactions that do not necessarily seem to be connected to your job or church. You may want to seek professional counseling if you are having persistent difficulties that make you identify with questions like these:

1. Do you feel you are at fault regardless of where you are or whom you are with?
2. Do you blame others for the bad things that happen to you, always feeling like you are a "victim"?

3. Do you feel anger or resentment toward someone you cannot forgive?
4. Do you fantasize about hurting someone and getting revenge for something he or she has done to you?
5. Do you bury your pain and deny it?
6. Do you react without any understanding of why you do what you do?
7. Do you overreact when you don't get your way or when others don't see things your way?

These are just some of the emotional and behavioral patterns that disrupt people's lives and that will cause problems regardless of whether you're at home, on the job or at church. In addition to those just highlighted by the series of questions, there are other types of personality patterns. In chapter 4 we will consider the codependent personality, and in chapter 5 the demonically influenced personality. You may want to look ahead to see if and how either or both of these might apply to your situation. However, as important as working on any of these with a counselor may be, it does not take the place of working through the recovery process outlined in this book. In fact, it is entirely possible to do both at the same time, and doing them in that way may even be desirable.

Nevertheless, dysfunctional personality patterns of workers do not negate the fact that there are dysfunctional organizational patterns. And when the two are combined it is often not a pretty sight. In the next two chapters you will learn more about recognizing negative patterns in your organization and in your own life. This will lay the groundwork for you to make an informed and confident decision regarding your future in your organization.

Unraveling the Addictive Organization

PASTOR ED WAS IN TROUBLE. As the charismatic leader of a large evangelical church, he had greatly expanded the ministry by enlisting many unbelievers into the cause of Christ. He had also greatly enlarged the church facilities to make room for many needed new programs and to be prepared for future growth. But when he decided to fire the music director and hire the unqualified, attractive, young female children's choir director as the replacement, people began to talk. "There's more here than meets the eye," they said. Pastor Ed, it seemed, had some explaining to do.

Pastor Ed began his damage control with a verbal defense to the board. He had let the music director go, he maintained, because he didn't like the songs that the music director had been choosing for the Sunday morning worship services. Furthermore, there was friction between the music director and the worship leader, who personally disliked the music director. As for the attractive, young choir director, she was a friend of the family and she could learn on the job. Enough said.

People continued to talk. Pastor Ed and the young choir director were spending a lot of time together at the church, weren't they? They hadn't done anything wrong, as far as anyone knew, but it still had the appearance of evil. The clamor began to filter back to members of the church board. They didn't like hearing that their pastor might be engaging in immoral activities. It was nothing more than gossip, so they decided to put a stop to it. They warned that anyone who continued to question the pastor regarding his dealings with staff personnel would be unbiblically challenging his authority and would therefore be disciplined by the church.

Tim, the associate pastor of the church, was very upset that his good friend, the music director, had been fired. He could not just sit back and pretend that everything was okay, "singing the Lord's song in a strange land." He had to defend his friend and expose the injustice done to him.

It also upset Tim how Pastor Ed was again, as in the past, being sheltered and protected by his board. Tim knew Ed quite well and knew that he had grown up as the family "hero." Ed always needed to be right—he was a perfectionist—and he needed to be venerated. Now he was being kept from being accountable to those he supposedly served. He could deny there was a problem with the firing or that he had done anything wrong, because the board kept him from hearing it.

Tim decided to confront Ed in spite of the board's warning. What he found was not the Ed that most people knew or thought they knew. In his pastoral duties, Ed liked to be on center stage and draw attention to himself, as the man who was running the show. But out of the limelight, he was completely detached from it all. Tim discovered that ministry meant nothing to him, that it was all a "con." This was not the enthusiastic, warm and caring individual that everyone knew on Sundays.

To Tim's astonishment, Ed admitted to him that he had no love for the people of the church. In fact, his one true desire was to become district superintendent, so he could still run the show but from a distance. His purpose for developing such an apparently successful church was only so that he could get his promotion.

Tim could not get the phrase "wolf in sheep's clothing" out of his mind. Scripture tells us to beware of those who come in sheep's clothing but inwardly are ravenous wolves.[1] Tim knew that this warning is not about followers (the sheep) but about leaders (the shepherds). The problem is not a bunch of sheep trying to destroy the church. Rather, the real problem is the shepherd, who is in a position to devour the sheep by satisfying his hunger for personal gain. Tim knew that in his church's case, Scripture was not warning about people being troublemakers and questioning authority. He knew the real issue was their misplaced trust in Pastor Ed, who was not shepherding but was satisfying his hunger for personal gain.

After the initial and subsequent confrontations between Tim and Pastor Ed, Tim could sense the pastor withdrawing his support. Pastor Ed finally insisted that Tim submit to the board's directive or be subject to discipline. The fire was lit, and Tim was on the skewer.

Tim was confused, depressed, frustrated and angry. He became paranoid regarding what was going to happen to him. He lost his self-confidence and a good deal of his self-esteem. He gradually became estranged from everything that was going on. His anger was all that kept him going. It was a hopeless situation.

The story of Pastor Ed and Tim is a story about a neurotic organization. Neurotic organizations, however, can also be viewed from an entirely different perspective. According to some researchers, dramatic, compulsive, suspicious, depressive and detached organizations are also *addictive organizations*.[2]

For example, looking at the leader, organization and wounded worker in the story of Ed and Tim, we can readily pick out features of the addictive personality. There are the self-dramatization, self-centeredness and mood swings (from enthusiasm to emotional detachment) in Pastor Ed. There are the perfectionism of the pastor, the board's preoccupation with control, and the compulsive behavior of both the pastor and the board.

There are the frozen feelings of Pastor Ed and the paranoia of Tim. There are Tim's feelings of depression and inadequacy. And finally there is Tim's estrangement from the entire situation.

CHARACTERISTICS OF AN ADDICTIVE SYSTEM

In addition to revealing elements that are both neurotic and addictive, our story of Ed and Tim contains features that are especially descriptive of an addictive process. The board sheltered and protected Ed just like a classic codependent would. Because of it, Ed was kept in denial and did not face the problem he was causing the church. In addition, he added to the unreality of it all by conning everyone into thinking he was somebody he was not.

Tim also added to the picture of addiction we see in our story. He used the "fix" of anger just to keep going. The whole situation was very confusing, and that is a vital element of an addictive system. In an addictive system, everyone is trying to figure out what is happening. Everyone is trying to predict what is going to happen next. All kinds of controls are in place to control what happens next. And, because of the controls, no one is able to get what he or she really needs. Tim was caught in the middle. So, in addition to being angry, he was paranoid and knew there wasn't a thing he could do about it.

We used a psychoanalytic framework in chapter 3 to describe the neurotic organization. Switching to more of a systems approach to describe the addictive organization enables us to view the organization as more than the sum of its parts. Systems are overarching entities that are more than composites of leaders, leadership styles, organizational cultures and workers. They provide a view of the whole—of the interactions of all of the parts. Understanding the system helps us make sense of our experience and understand what is going on around us.

Systems are either open or closed. Open systems are flexible. They welcome new information and change. Closed systems, on the other hand, are rigid. New information must fit in with the system as it stands, or it will not be recognized; it will not even be seen as existing. Addictive systems are closed systems.

Life inside the closed system of the addictive organization is governed by several processes that hook people into addictive relationships with the organization. I want to consider seven of them.[3]

1. **Co-opting**. This is the process of absorbing and utilizing anything that is different but potentially useful. The hitch is that the system does not allow the incorporation of the new and different idea or method to upset the status quo. For example, suppose church members cry out for more opportunities to actively participate in worship instead of sitting passively as spectators. So, the church leadership allows them to pick some hymns and stand more often while singing. The leaders can now proclaim that they have "participatory" worship services, but truly meaningful change has not yet taken place.

2. **Tokenism**. This is superficially and minimally responding to a problem. Suppose church members ask for more opportunities for women to participate in church governance. So, the church leaders appoint one of the women to be a pastor for women, but do not allow any women to serve on the governing board. Again, nothing has really changed.

3. **External referencing**. This simply means that organizations operate in terms of how persons outside the organization perceive them. In Christian organizations, this usually refers to the constituency. In the worst-case scenario, there are no organizational boundaries: If it pleases the constituents, do it; if it doesn't, don't. It feels good. It feels safe.

An excellent example is the experience some years ago of a seminary student who spoke out against the Vietnam War. He was called in to speak with the president, and this is what he was told:

> It's not that we don't trust your sincerity and integrity. It's not that your concerns are unbiblical. . . . It's just that the presence of you and your friends has cost the seminary almost a million dollars in lost contributions. . . .
>
> If you continue to act and speak out against the war, against the government, against the things America stands for, we will have no choice but to dismiss you from school. Our financial needs will require it. . . . We just can't afford to keep you here.[4]

The seminary student's concerns were not unbiblical, but they were perceived as "against the things America stands for." What an example that is of the addictive process of selling out. Fortunately, the student was not hooked into an addictive relationship with the seminary. But the president regrettably was, by a very powerful addictive substance indeed: money. How easy it is for a Christian organization to drop its biblical boundaries because their "financial needs" require it.

4. **Invalidation.** Christian organizations are particularly vulnerable to this addictive process. Invalidation is defining out of existence any ideas or experiences that are threatening. In the interest of doctrinal purity, certain things just cannot be allowed to exist. For example, in a strongly dispensational church, some of the spiritual gifts listed in Scripture do not exist today. They cannot. Indoctrination makes sure of it.

5. **Exaggerating personality conflicts**. This process magnifies the fact that the bearers of unwanted information are in conflict with one another, if in fact that can be used against them. Since they are in disagreement among themselves, it is pointed out, the issue doesn't need to be taken seriously. For example, if a group of people are dissatisfied with the pastor but are not in agreement concerning his inadequacies, it is fairly easy for the board to say, "They're just squabbling among themselves. What some don't like others do and vice versa. Surely the Lord can't be in that."

6. **Dualistic thinking**. This process simplifies everything down to just two choices. For Christians, those choices are often good and evil. The rigidity that this creates eliminates the need and the ability to consider other options. It's either right or wrong, good or evil, and that's all there is to it. But when something comes along that can't easily be relegated to one or the other category, people get stuck—they cannot think for themselves.

7. **Trusting the promise**. Just like an addict's loved ones, an addictive organization will hold out hope that things will get better. The hoped-for glory in the future serves as a great relief from the wounds of the present. It is a fix, a very powerful fix.

The promise of the future is especially powerful in Christian organizations. For example, if we are being told that we should expect to be underpaid while working in a Christian organization, then we are often also told that God's work has its own rewards and that in heaven we will get our reward. This reasoning is very powerful, because the bit about getting our reward in heaven is true. But it is powerful for another reason as well:

> The future orientation of the promise in the organization is one of the processes that prevent us from looking at the present functioning in the system and seeing it for exactly what it is . . . . By continuing to present us with the promise, the organization remains central in our lives, in control of our present, and "hooks" us into an addictive relationship with the organization, the giver of the promise.[5]

There are primarily three different ways in which the power of the promise operates within an addictive organization. The first is when the organization is conceived of as a *family*. This brings into the life of the organization all of the dynamics of the addictive family. People are accepted not for who they are, but for whether they do the right thing. In this family, love is conditional—but love should be unconditional, especially if it is a Christian family. Love, however, is not the basis for addictive family life; control is.

In the addictive organization (or family), people do whatever it takes to stay in the organization's good graces. If you want to have a future, you must play by the rules. If you won't sacrifice your own needs, you're out. Certainly the organization's promise to be a family is a mixed blessing, to say the least.

The second way in which the organization's promise operates is when it is stated in the organizational *mission*. The reason many people are attracted to Christian organizations is that such organizations are often intentionally Christ-centered and inspired by the highest ideals—those given by God through Scripture. Especially when the implementation of these ideals is spelled out in a God-breathed mission statement, it is easy to see how it can hook Christian workers.

There is a downside however: The mission of the organization is so lofty and so full of promise for the future that it masks the reality of present discrepancies. The loftier the mission becomes, the more excuses are made, and the more people pretend to be doing more than they really are. The mission itself becomes a fix. It makes them feel good, because what they are doing seems to be so important in God's eyes, even though they are not getting done what they should be getting done. Perhaps they are furthering their own kingdom, but they are not very effectively furthering God's kingdom. And in their state of denial, they are just too heavenly minded to do any earthly good.

The third way in which the organization's promise operates is through *benefits*. Medical insurance, bonuses, housing allowances, tenure, stock options—all of these can become fixes in an addictive system. The promise of benefits is not a bad thing, but it can have the wrong effects. Benefits can become the sole motivation for keeping a job, and they can contribute greatly to creating and sustaining an addictive organization.

People who do not want to stay but who do so anyway, often do so because they are afraid to leave for fear of losing their benefits. Just as often, they become neutralized in their effectiveness and numbed to the promptings of the Holy Spirit regarding the injustices around them. They may also begin to function within the system totally for self gain. If it means more benefits, they will do it, whatever it takes and however unbecoming of a Christian it may be. This might help explain why we hear so often about various unethical and immoral acts taking place within Christian organizations. Those involved did it to get ahead, without admitting to themselves that it was wrong as they were doing it. Just like an addict.

Workaholism

While benefits can become fixes, working to obtain them can as well. Perhaps for this reason we should be careful as we look at incentives to increase productivity. The work itself can provide a fix just like the benefit can because of the adrenaline high that accompanies the work. For some, to work is to be alive and full of energy. To take a vacation or to suffer through a weekend, however, is to be bored and tired—unalive.

Perhaps we should also look closely at the issue of stress in the workplace. If you treat stress as the problem and teach yourself to eat right, exercise daily, and so forth, it could play right into the larger problem of work addiction. By becoming able to work harder and longer, you also become able to ruin your life in other ways (by ignoring friends and family, making money your god, eliminating all nonwork-related activities, etc.). Here's more food for thought:

> The insidious thing is that their stress reduction activities appear to be promoting health when, in actuality, these activities only allow workaholics to prolong their addiction—taking the focus off their addiction, actually supporting their addiction, and serving as a con for themselves and others. It appears that stress research and stress reduction workshops may indeed actually be supporting the perpetuation of the addictive system.[6]

Addictive organizations thrive on workaholism. They reward workaholic behavior. Whether through bonuses, incentive programs or stress-reduction workshops, they are reinforcing the addiction process. They are becoming the center of workers' lives, while numbing them to their own pain and nurturing their denial as to its cause. The wound of the workers is that they are being used and do not know it.

Many churches thrive on workaholism. It is not usually their intent to do so, and it can develop quite unexpectedly. A common core value across all church denominations is to work hard. Coupled with that core value, in many cases, is an unstated expectation to work selflessly, without attending to personal needs. When backed by the authority of the Bible, this creates a foothold for workaholism.

As workaholism begins to take hold within the organizational culture, it begins to challenge another common core value, which is to grow spiritually. When workaholism gathers a full head of steam, it produces in individuals a kind of mood-altering state—a feeling of transcendence somewhat like a "spiritual high." *True* spirituality, regrettably, is replaced by a feeling, under the guise of good works. Experiencing God is replaced by expecting God to provide for the habit. Workaholism has become, in reality, the drug of choice for the church as well as for the corporation.

PUTTING YOUR ORGANIZATION TO THE TEST

Let's find out how addictive your organization is. Do you work or worship in a place that leaves you with the wound of *religious addiction*? Have you become dependent on the organization through its various addictive processes? Is your ear deaf to the voice of God speaking into your life and your eye blind to the fix of work that is ruining your life?

The following test will help you understand what might be wrong with your organization.[7] This test has the same format as the similar test in chapter 3, and it also has not been scientifically validated. However, the information from the test—together with the background information about the characteristics of an addictive system that was presented in the preceding material—will help you do the following:

1. Understand what may not be "normal" and what must be changed in your organization.
2. Appreciate that perhaps your problem is not just *your* problem.

Place an X in the *Always, Sometimes,* or *Never* column for each item—whichever applies to you and your organization.

ORGANIZATION TEST: ADDICTIVE

	Always	*Sometimes*	*Never*
1. Do you spend your weekends recovering from the emotional exhaustion of work?	☐	☐	☐

	Always	Sometimes	Never
2. Is communication at work vague and indirect, and are people unwilling to express conflicts openly with those who are most involved?	☐	☐	☐
3. If you express your feelings, will you be seen as unstable and jeopardize your job security?	☐	☐	☐
4. Does the leadership blame the economy, the competition or Satan for its own failures?	☐	☐	☐
5. Is the illusion of perfection upheld through denial and dishonesty?	☐	☐	☐
6. Is there a sense that everything revolves around the organization, almost like it's the center of the universe?	☐	☐	☐
7. Is there an air of judgmentalism, where even gossip has an intent to hurt and defame?	☐	☐	☐
8. Do you spend an inordinate amount of time trying to figure out what is going on?	☐	☐	☐
9. Are new ideas or ways of doing things adopted, but nothing really changes?	☐	☐	☐

	Always	Sometimes	Never
10. Do you find yourself getting on bandwagons or being pulled into things you do not feel right about?	❏	❏	❏
11. Do you work only for the benefits?	❏	❏	❏
12. Is the constituency manipulated to believe certain things and take actions that favor the organization or its leaders?	❏	❏	❏
13. Are personnel practices built around the supposed goodness or badness of the person rather than the consequences of choices made?	❏	❏	❏
14. Are you underpaid and being told that your reward will be in heaven?	❏	❏	❏
15. Is information withheld, and then when someone goes out on a limb and complains about something, he or she is made to feel like a fool with the comment, "Your complaint isn't valid, and you'd know that if you had all the information"?	❏	❏	❏
16. Do you feel there is undue competition for rewards and recognition?	❏	❏	❏

	Always	Sometimes	Never

17. Do you feel the "form as a fix" syndrome is operating, whereby a person who has a problem is given, in every case, a spiritual solution, and everyone but the person with the problem feels better?

18. Do you see "quick fixes"— getting rid of the problem by firing people who have a "poor attitude" or who are "insubordinate," or by becoming militant about defending doctrinal purity?

19. Do you find options for individual thinking and behaving limited by the "company line," political correctness or subculturalism (the controlling commandments, code words and political agenda of the Evangelical— or other—subculture)?

20. Does it seem that when something negative happens, it's almost as though the existence of the entire organization is threatened?

21. Do you find that what your organization is committed to and what you experience are quite different?

	Always	Sometimes	Never
22. Does the organization pretend to be more than it is?	❑	❑	❑
23. Are you constantly vigilant about what you need to do to stay in good graces and gain approval?	❑	❑	❑
24. Does it seem like the organization does whatever its constituency wants it to do?	❑	❑	❑
25. Are meetings dominated by mundane announcements, success stories and superficial prayer requests, to the exclusion of prayerful discussion of deeply rooted problems that may threaten the future of the organization?	❑	❑	❑

If you answered *Always* or *Sometimes* to ten or more of the questions, then you are probably in an addictive organization. You now have more information to help you understand why it is an unpleasant place to work or worship. If you are in such a situation, the next test will help you begin to understand what you should do about it.

PUTTING YOURSELF TO THE TEST

How do you contribute to your own woundedness? Let's take a look, as we did in the previous chapter, at what you, with your personality, might be bringing to wherever you work or worship that makes matters worse.

The following questions relate your personality to the addictive organization.[8] Opposite each one place an X in the *Yes* column if it applies to you or in the *No* column if it does not. Answer each question in terms of how it relates to *your personality in general*, not your present situation.

SELF TEST

	Yes	No
1. Do you tend to severely criticize yourself to neutralize any praise you might receive?	☐	☐
2. Is it difficult for you to say no?	☐	☐
3. Do you think in black-and-white terms?	☐	☐
4. Are you most calm when things are falling apart?	☐	☐
5. Are you a poor team player?	☐	☐
6. Do you need lots of encouragement and personal approval, and when you do not get it, do you react with anger and hostility?	☐	☐
7. Does your sense of worth come primarily from being liked by others?	☐	☐
8. Are you adept at maintaining and perpetuating situations long after they should have come to an end?	☐	☐
9. Do you spend a good deal of your time trying to understand and care for the needs of others and picking up on subtle cues about what others expect from you?	☐	☐
10. Do you have trouble with boundaries?	☐	☐

Which items on the Self Test have marks in the *Yes* column? Which items on the Organization Test have marks in the *Always* or *Sometimes* columns? When you put them together for comparison, what do they tell you?

Are your personality characteristics only reinforcing your situation? Does what you bring to the situation make it worse? Does the interaction of your personality and your organization's weaknesses say something about whether you should try to be a change agent in your job or church? Should you stay, or should you leave?

Codependent Personality

You may have noticed when you were going over the test items that many of the items describe codependency and adult children of alcoholics. Codependency is probably the most readily identifiable personality characteristic in addictive organizations.

For example, what if on the Self Test you marked *Yes* to "Is it difficult to say no?" "Does your sense of worth come primarily from being liked by others?" "Are you adept at maintaining and perpetuating situations long after they should have come to an end?" "Do you spend a good deal of your time trying to understand and care for the needs of others and picking up on subtle cues about what others expect from you?" and "Do you have trouble with boundaries?"

What if on the Organization Test you marked *Always* to "Are personnel practices built around the supposed goodness or badness of the person rather than the consequences of choices made?" and "Are you constantly vigilant about what you need to do to stay in good graces and gain approval?"

These responses basically define the codependent personality. You are bringing the very qualities to the organization that the organization, being the type that it is, is making worse. You are going to have a very hard time in that organization.

You may want to gather more information through further reading to see what more, if anything, you may need to do for recovery in this area of woundedness.[9] You may also want to look back to chapter 3 and look ahead to chapter 5 to consider any dysfunctional personality characteristics or demonically influenced personality characteristics, respectively, that you might have. How might they affect your stay in the addictive organization you may have discovered your organization to be? This will be useful information to have when we get to chapters 8–10, where we will take up directly the question of whether you should remain where you are or remove yourself from the organization.

Unmasking the Spiritually Abusive Organization

IN CHAPTER 4, WE MET PASTOR ED. He was a charismatic preacher who was warm and caring on Sunday but cold and out of touch on Monday. He cared more about being promoted to district superintendent than he did about loving people. He was a wolf in sheep's clothing.

Jesus warned us, "Beware of false prophets, who come to you in sheep's clothing but inwardly are ravenous wolves."[1] The apostle Paul picked up the warning in his farewell to the elders of the church in Ephesus: "I know that after I leave, savage wolves will come in among you and will not spare the flock. Even from your own number men will arise and distort the truth in order to draw away disciples after them."[2]

This theme runs throughout Scripture. In the Old Testament, the prophet Ezekiel warns about it also: "Her officials within her are like wolves tearing their prey; they shed blood and kill people to make unjust gain."[3] Not holding back, Ezekiel puts it to them:

> Is it not enough for you to feed on the good pasture? Must you
> also trample the rest of your pasture with your feet? Is it not
> enough for you to drink clear water? Must you also muddy the
> rest with your feet? Must my flock feed on what you have
> trampled and drink what you have muddied with your feet?[4]

Scripture confronts the leaders: Don't defile and destroy the sheep, don't flatten the grass, and don't foul the water. Don't corrupt the spiritual life of others to satisfy your own craving for influence and personal fulfillment. Don't feed yourself at the expense of abusing those you are supposed to serve.

We have a name for this spiritual masquerading and manipulation: It is *spiritual abuse*. In chapter 4 we discussed systems that abuse by being addictive. Similarly, there are systems that abuse spiritually—two sides of the same coin. What is unique about spiritually abusive systems is the weakening of one person's empowerment in order to strengthen another person's position, as expressed in the following:

> There are spiritual systems in which what people think, how
> they feel and what they need or want does not matter. People's
> needs go unmet. In these systems, the members are there to
> meet the needs of the leaders: needs for power, importance,
> intimacy, value—really, *self*-related needs. These leaders attempt
> to find fulfillment through the religious performance of the very
> people whom they are there to serve and build. This is an
> inversion in the body of Christ. It is spiritual abuse.[5]

The followers are there to meet the needs of the leaders. That's the key. In spiritually abusive systems, leaders basically find fulfillment through the enhancement of their reputation that comes from the religious performance of others. They also need an organization that does all the "right" things. Above all else, these leaders must always come off looking good, regardless of the situation. But in order to do that, sooner or later they have to mistreat people or spiritually abuse them.

Spiritual abuse occurs when the leader uses his or her position of authority to force others to live up to a spiritual standard, without regard for the individual's spiritual well-being. And quite often there is equal disregard for the biblical authenticity of the standard. The individual must prove his or her spiritual worthiness by living up to that standard, in order to bolster the position and needs of the leader.

Listen as a young lady talks about a premarriage counseling session with her pastor:

> "I simply asked him what he thought about me taking a job outside the home after we got married. I was so surprised at his answer. His face turned red, his lips drew thin, and he appeared almost angry. He said I should not even get married if I was considering working outside the home. As a Christian wife, my life was to be in the home and with the children. Further, he said that if I was not planning to have kids right away, I should definitely not get married at all. I felt ashamed for even having brought it up."

Another woman in the same church had this to say:

> "I was asked to chair a committee to rewrite the church constitution. We need a new constitution very badly, particularly because of the unilateral powers given to the church board and the pastor, who is the chairman of the board. Those board members aren't accountable to the membership at all, because they're appointed for life. I knew that had to change, but I also knew they would never accept a change in the constitution that limited their power. So I asked for the provision that a working draft be presented to the entire church membership, at the same time as the board, for discussion. They were adamant that they must see it first and okay it before letting the church members see it. They would not back down. They didn't want my best effort—they wanted me to be a puppet. It was so belittling. I quit."

A third situation in the same church also came to my attention. One of the members had acquired evidence of financial and operational irregularities perpetrated by the church leadership. He presented his findings to the pastor and then to the board, but neither was receptive to discussing the matter. So, he requested permission to present his case to the church body, and a congregational meeting was arranged:

> "I can't believe what happened at that meeting. The pastor read through some of the items I'd come up with, but I was not allowed to bring up the ones he left out. Some of the people there had copies, but others didn't, so there was a lot of confusion. There was no real discussion. Then pre-printed ballots were given out with one yes or no choice on it for the statement, 'I have complete confidence in the pastor and board.' I know some people had trouble with the word 'complete,' and others couldn't understand what they were doing. There had not been a balanced presentation, and nothing had been discussed regarding the relative merits of the two positions. Also, a couple of outsiders were brought in to attack my character. It was very unfair.
>
> "Well, I sat through that and the nearly unanimous vote against me personally—which was not the issue at hand—and then got more the following Sunday at the morning service. The pastor used his entire sermon to attack me again, all the time saying that he was not angry, but he could hardly talk he was so angry. Again, I was not given a chance to say a word, and my family and I just had to sit through that and take it. From then on we were effectively shunned and had to leave the church in disgrace. What did we do? Just raise some questions, and that's what we got!"

When Jesus saw situations like these, he had compassion, "because they were harassed and helpless, like sheep without a shepherd"—or as another translation puts it, "because they were like shepherdless sheep that are mangled and thrown to the ground."[6] Sheep do not have the power of shepherds. Even if the lady with the constitution and the man at the congregational meeting had been bent on destroying the fellowship—which they were not—they could not have succeeded nearly as well at that as could the leadership. Sheep can *disrupt*, but shepherds can *devour*.

Shepherds have the power of authority. Sheep have only the prickle of complaint.

CHARACTERISTICS OF A SPIRITUALLY ABUSIVE SYSTEM

What do spiritually abusive organizations have in common? Although there are numerous characteristics, I will list seven. Characteristics one through four describe the forces that dictate how people must behave, while five through seven describe the forces that make it so hard for people to escape.[7]

1. Power-posturing

Leaders spend lots of time focusing on their authority, and reminding others of it. They are over-eager to place people under them—under the "mantle" or the "covering" of their authority. Many use the power of the pulpit to position themselves as the authority. They use the worship service as a mere front for their own ego. They subordinate every other element of the service to the preaching—all singing, praying and Scripture reading are merely preliminary and subordinate to the focal point namely the sermon. This ministerial monopoly, the undue predominance of one man conducting the service, gives the impression of a master of ceremonies. The "worship" service is a projection of the pastor's personality rather than the practice of the presence of God.

Many spiritually abusive leaders also use Scripture to keep the focus of the congregation on who is in charge and who is to obey. Let's look at that more closely, with help from an authoritative source on spiritual abuse:

> Hebrews 13:17 states: "Obey your leaders, and submit to them; for they keep watch over your souls, as those who give an account." In abusive systems, however, that verse is stripped of its spirit and translated legalistically to mean, "Don't think, don't discern, don't question, and don't notice problems." If you do, you will be labeled as unsubmissive, unspiritual, and divisive.
>
> The fact of the matter is that while we should give "double honor" to those elders who "rule well" (I Timothy 5:17), not all

elders *rule well*. Spiritual leaders are people who prove over the
long run that they know how to lead souls to peace.[8]

What we need to remember is that true authority is not obtained
through intense posturing and intimidating proclamations. Rather,
it is received as a gift, and it is recognized by the fruitfulness of its
ministry. In a word, authority is given, not grasped. Notice the
following emphasis on the Giver rather than the recipient:

> In Matthew 28:18 Jesus says, "All authority *has been given* to Me
> in heaven and on earth." Matthew 10:1 says, "And having
> summoned His twelve disciples, He *gave them* authority." Being
> hired or elected to a spiritual position, talking the loudest, or
> giving the most does not give someone authority. God does give
> it, and He does so for the purpose of coming underneath people
> in the body of Christ to build them, serve them, equip them and
> set them free to do God's agenda—which may or may not
> coincide with the agenda of the leadership.[9]

2. Performance preoccupation

Obedience and submission are overly emphasized and backed
up by shaming techniques. You must play by the rules to gain
approval, maintain or grow in spiritual stature, and give the church
and its leadership a good name. But God calls us to obedience to
His good name, above all other names. He does not call us to a
legislated obedience that is nothing more than the promotion of
oneself and the organization. Again, let's look more closely at this
issue:

> Are obedience and submission important? Without question.
> This can be seen in Romans 13:1: "Let every person be in
> subjection to the governing authorities." And 1 Peter 5:5 says,
> "Be subject to your elders." Hebrews 13:17 also says,
> emphatically, "Obey your leaders, and submit to them." To bring
> balance, however, we must add to these verses an equally
> important passage. Consider the words of Peter and the other
> apostles in Acts 5:29: "We must obey God rather than men."
> Notice that Peter is saying this to the religious leaders he was

disobeying. Out of context, obedience to leaders looks like good theology. Add the larger context, and you will see that *it is only appropriate to obey and submit to leadership when their authority is from God and their stance is consistent with His.*[10]

3. Unspoken rules

These are just as powerful in governing people's behavior as are the legislated rules that the leaders keep rehearsing over and over again. When it is not directly stated that you had better not discuss the undiscussables (as defined in chapter 1: the secrets that everyone knows about but is afraid to bring up), but you get nailed for it when you do, it is pretty powerful indeed.

When the man presented earlier—who tried to bring to light certain irregularities perpetrated by the church leadership—broke the code of silence, he was punished. He was victimized by how the congregational meeting was conducted, yet he was seen as the problem and was shunned right out of the church. This form of punishment is called, aptly, *blaming the victim.*

4. Lack of balance

When there is abuse in the system, there is one of two extremes. Either objective truth is elevated to the exclusion of valid subjective experience, or it is the other way around. I call these two extremes *bibliolatry* and *charismania*, respectively.

Bibliolatry is the belief that nothing is true if it cannot be found in the Bible. Therefore, we must live our lives exactly in accordance with the objective words of Scripture—to the letter. However, since subjective experience is not considered to play any positive role whatsoever in knowing truth, it is not acknowledged as part of the process of reading and understanding what the Bible has to say. This creates a problem.

Without an understanding that personal factors can enter into the reading of the Bible—unconscious motivations, conscious biases, even distorted perceptual abilities—then how are we to explain the perversions of the Bible concocted by cults? They read the same Bible that we do. Or what about the less extreme example of disagreements among denominations over certain passages of Scripture, or the fact that we continually find new insights and applications as we read the same Bible through the course of our lifetime? The Bible is the same, but we are not.

Where there is extreme objectivism, there is abuse. This happens, for example, when the leadership holds tenaciously to its interpretation of the Bible regarding how everyone should live their lives. No challenges to the leadership's interpretation are allowed. No exceptions to a strict, biblically derived behavioral code that covers every detail of a person's life can be tolerated. The Bible replaces God as the focus and therefore becomes an idol. Fear replaces faith. And when that happens, there will be abuse.

Charismania is just as bad. Where there is extreme subjectivism there is also abuse. If everyone believes their ultimate authority is a private word from God, they will be going off in all different directions. Chaos gets abusive. When a leader takes over and claims that the ultimate direction of the group and the individual members' lives is subject only to the leader's direct revelation from God, the stage is set for even greater abuse. It becomes a closed system, where the leader's subjective experience cannot be challenged with Scripture. And there are penalties for trying.

5. Paranoia

This is the first of three characteristics that describe the forces that make it so difficult for victims to escape from spiritually abusive systems. It can be called "cultural paranoia" and is similar to that found in the neurotic organization described in chapter 3. In the spiritually abusive organization, paranoia permeates the culture primarily in the form of expecting criticism and avoiding contamination, as we can see in the following:

> There is a sense, spoken or unspoken, that "others will not understand what we're all about, so let's not let them know—that way they won't be able to ridicule or persecute us." There is an assumption that (1) what you say, know or do is a result of being more enlightened than others; (2) others will not

understand unless they become one of your own; and (3) they otherwise will respond negatively.

In a place where authority is grasped and legislated, not simply demonstrated, persecution sensitivity builds a case for keeping everything within the system. Why? Because of the evil, dangerous, or unspiritual people outside of the system who are trying to weaken or destroy "us." This mentality builds a strong wall or bunker around the abusive system, isolates the abusers from scrutiny and accountability, and makes it more difficult for people to leave—because they will then be outsiders too. While it is true that there is a world of evil outside of the system, there is also good out there. But people are misled into thinking that the *only* safety is in the system.[11]

6. Misplaced loyalty

Simply put, this is loyalty to the company, to the church, or to a leader rather than to Christ. This is also part of the culture, because it is demanded by the leadership. They do not actually say that you must be loyal to them *instead of* to Christ. But they do say that if you disagree with them then you are disobeying God. They might just as well come right out and say it: "Don't obey God or what you think God is telling you. Obey us."

It's hard to break away from this. After all, the leadership is always right. It doesn't matter what you read in Scripture or how the Holy Spirit seems to be leading you. The risk is too great to consider leaving—and being wrong.

Punishment can get pretty severe when you are "exposed" for being disloyal. It may take the form of being told that God will not bless your family or your business. Or you may be made into a public example in order to keep others in line. That is exactly what happened to the man mentioned earlier who tried to present evidence against the church leadership at a congregational meeting, and was victimized and humiliated both at the meeting and at the worship service the following Sunday. But the pastor did even more than was mentioned earlier. He actually phoned the man's customers to talk them out of doing business with him. The pastor attempted to ruin the man's business, because he dared to question the church leadership!

7. Secretiveness

Finally, the culture of the spiritually abusive organization is secretive. Again, it is difficult to leave such an organization—because of the addictiveness of the conspiracies that develop. The positive feelings of inclusion when involved in a conspiracy are very powerful.

The unwritten rule about discussing undiscussables is also in place, of course, so there is a sort of collusion of codependents. Behind closed doors, at lunch and over the telephone, everything gets cussed and discussed. But to no avail. It all goes nowhere. The workers are working hard on their own personal kingdoms, but God's kingdom is on hold. Sound familiar?

PUTTING YOUR ORGANIZATION TO THE TEST

Let's find out how spiritually abusive your organization is. Let's see if you have developed a "toxic faith" in your leader/organization, which allows them to inappropriately control your life in the name of God.[12]

The following test will help you understand what might be wrong with your organization.[13] This test is similar in format to the Organization Test in the previous two chapters. Again, it is not a scientifically validated test. However, the information from the test and the background information about the characteristics of a spiritually abusive system that was presented in the preceding material will help you:

1. Understand what may not be "normal" and what must be changed in your organization.
2. Appreciate that perhaps your problem is not just *your* problem.

Place an X in the *Always, Sometimes*, or *Never* column for each item—whichever applies to you and your organization.

ORGANIZATION TEST: SPIRITUALLY ABUSIVE

	Always	Sometimes	Never
1. Is loyalty to the organization or its leadership your number one concern?	☐	☐	☐
2. Do you have a distorted image of God—does He seem demanding and fickle?	☐	☐	☐
3. Do you have a distorted emphasis on spiritual performance—are you preoccupied with following the right formula so you will please God?	☐	☐	☐
4. Do you have a distorted self-identity—is shame the prime motivator of your behavior, so when you feel you don't measure up, you begin to feel defective as a human being and undeserving of the Lord's blessings?	☐	☐	☐
5. Do you have difficulty with authority—are you either extremely compliant or automatically defiant?	☐	☐	☐
6. Do you have difficulty with grace—do you reject living under grace as being lazy, as taking advantage of God or as getting off the hook?	☐	☐	☐

	Always	Sometimes	Never
7. Do you have difficulty with personal boundaries—are you easily shamed out of saying no, or have you been conned into believing that expressing a contrary opinion is a lack of submissiveness, especially if you are a woman?	☐	☐	☐
8. Do you have difficulty with responsibility—have you decided to let others carry on the work of the ministry, because you feel you just don't measure up?	☐	☐	☐
9. Do you have difficulty with social skills—have you been so closed off from the world that you cannot function outside your own little Christian ghetto?	☐	☐	☐
10. Do you have difficulty even considering the possibility of abuse—is it too painful to think in those terms, or do you hesitate to do so because if you bring up a problem you will be defined as the problem?	☐	☐	☐
11. Do you have difficulty with trust—are you becoming disillusioned in your faith and cynical toward spiritual matters?	☐	☐	☐

	Always	Sometimes	Never
12. Is authority seen as the primary ingredient of leadership?	☐	☐	☐
13. Are there lots of unspoken rules that keep people in line?	☐	☐	☐
14. Is the Bible used to control every moment of your life?	☐	☐	☐
15. Is the direction of the organization determined by private and personal divine revelation?	☐	☐	☐
16. Is there a sense that the only thing that people outside the organization do is ridicule your organization and what you are trying to accomplish?	☐	☐	☐
17. Is it really hard to leave, because you believe it is safe only where you are?	☐	☐	☐
18. If you disagree with the leadership, do you feel you are disagreeing with God?	☐	☐	☐
19. Are you afraid to leave, because you know you would be wrong?	☐	☐	☐
20. Is the leadership condescending and patronizing toward everyone?	☐	☐	☐

	Always	Sometimes	Never
21. Are you hesitant to leave, because you enjoy the conspiracies that occur periodically?	☐	☐	☐
22. When problems arise, is someone always immediately found to blame?	☐	☐	☐
23. Is no one ever allowed to do anything outside of his or her specific role?	☐	☐	☐
24. Must everyone, at all costs, keep up the image of the organization and make the leader look good?	☐	☐	☐
25. Is nothing as important as the survival of the organization?	☐	☐	☐

If you answered *Always* or *Sometimes* to ten or more of the questions, then you are probably in a spiritually abusive organization. Now, hopefully, it is much clearer why it is an undesirable place for you to work or worship. If that is the case, the next test will help you begin the process of doing something about it.

PUTTING YOURSELF TO THE TEST

Do you contribute to your own woundedness? Let's take a look, as we did in previous chapters, at what you, with your personality, bring to wherever it is that you work or worship. Does it make matters worse?

The following questions relate your personality to the spiritually abusive organization.[14] Opposite each one place an X in the *Yes* column if it applies to you or in the *No* column if it does not. Answer each question in terms of how it relates to *your personality in general*, not your present situation.

SELF TEST

		Yes	No
1.	Do you tend to allow others to take advantage of you?	☐	☐
2.	Do you have a faith that says God is more interested in what you do than who you are?	☐	☐
3.	Do you continually read other meanings into what people say?	☐	☐
4.	Is your church background one of sharp reaction against a strong emphasis on either using Scripture to guide your life or the validity of subjective experience in knowing God's will for your life?	☐	☐
5.	Do you tend to look for external enemies to blame when something goes wrong?	☐	☐
6.	Are you afraid to ever question authority?	☐	☐
7.	Do you like to manage others' impressions so things will look better than they actually are?	☐	☐
8.	Do you believe that you cannot be hurt emotionally if you are strong enough spiritually?	☐	☐

	Yes	No
9. Do you distrust any organization that is not Christian simply because it is not Christian?	☐	☐
10. Do you have low self-esteem?	☐	☐

Which items on the Self Test have marks in the *Yes* column? Which items on the Organization Test have marks in the *Always* or *Sometimes* columns? What do they tell you, when put together for comparison?

Did you happen to find a pattern that reminded you of the codependent personality discussed at the end of chapter 4? That would not be at all unusual, since codependence is so common in both addictive and abusive settings. For example, on the Self Test you would have marked *Yes* to "Do you tend to allow others to take advantage of you?" and "Do you like to manage others' impressions so things will look better than they actually are?"

On the Organization Test, you would have marked *Always* to "Is loyalty to the organization or its leadership your number one concern?" "Do you have difficulty with authority—are you either extremely compliant or automatically defiant?" "Do you have difficulty with personal boundaries—are you easily shamed out of saying no, or have you been conned into believing that expressing a contrary opinion is a lack of submissiveness, especially if you are a woman?" "Must everyone, at all costs, keep up the image of the organization and make the leader look good?" and "Is nothing as important as the survival of the organization?"

Considering again all of the items on both tests that you marked *Yes* and *Always*, are your personality characteristics only reinforcing your situation? Does what you bring to the situation make it worse? Does the interaction of your personality and your organization's weaknesses tell you anything about whether you should attempt to change things in your job or church? Does it help you decide whether you should check out?

Demonically Influenced Personality[15]

A spiritually abusive environment is not always that way solely from human design. Where there are lies and half-truths that distort biblical truth, there is often evidence of a type of satanic activity referred to as *strongholds*. A stronghold is defined as "an entrenched pattern of thought, an ideology, value or behavior that is contrary to the word and will of God."[16] Strongholds operate at both the corporate and individual level.

We will consider organizational strongholds in chapter 9. At this point you need to look at yourself. Are you aware of things like fear, doubt, self-pity, jealousy, bitterness, hatred or a besetting sin that could be providing a foothold for demonic influence in your life? Footholds invite strongholds into your personality—moods become habits, inclinations become addictions, and a moment becomes a way of life. Strongholds are not actually demons but "trace to the unsanctified self—those parts of us not yet yielded to the Spirit or healed by grace."[17] It is in these areas that we think we don't need God, or think we do but don't do anything about it. We put ourselves in charge of our own destiny, and that is where Satan, the father of lies, does his handiwork. It is our self-will that is the chief source of spiritual strongholds.

How does one identify strongholds? Try this brief test:[18]

1. Do you see any attitudes, habits, or behaviors in your life that create ongoing cycles of defeat and seem to be avenues for enemy influence?
2. Do you wrestle with distorted messages (negative self-talk) concerning your identity and personal value?
3. Do you struggle with believing and receiving the Lord's love?
4. Do you experience uncontrolled feelings of envy, intimidation, fear, anger, criticism, etc., toward others?

A thread running through these four questions is an entrenched pattern of unforgiveness, which is contrary to the work and will of God. Being unforgiving of self and others and not accepting God's forgiveness are perhaps the strongest of all the strongholds. In contrast to God, Satan condemns the whole person—by planting inner thoughts of inadequacy and unworthiness that bring the person to a complete standstill. The Holy Spirit, on the other hand, convicts the person about something that is wrong (either because of commission or omission) and then empowers the person to do something about it.

Are you a victim or a captive? If you feel you might be captive to demonic influence and want to break the stronghold or strongholds in your life, then you will need more background information and instruction on what actions to take.[19] You might also review the victim side of the equation by taking a look back at the material given about the dysfunctional personality at the end of chapter 3, and the codependent personality at the end of chapter 4. This will give you a much more complete overview of what you bring to your situation that quite possibly is making it worse.

In chapters 8–10, we will look at your options, regardless of whether your organization is spiritually abusive or you have given it a clean bill of health. Whatever the case and whatever you have discovered about your organization and yourself in all of Phase One of the recovery process, here is a word of hope. The prophet Ezekiel, referred to earlier in this chapter, warned about wolves in sheep's clothing. But he then went on to tell how the Lord will save His flock and bless them and make them secure. Speaking to Israel, He also speaks to believers today: "And they shall know that I, the Lord their God, am with them, and that they, the house of Israel, are my people, says the Lord God. And you are my sheep, the sheep of my pasture, and I am your God, says the Lord God."[20]

You are His sheep, the sheep of His pasture! He will save you and bless you and keep you.

PHASE
TWO

REMEMBERING

Doing a Biblical
Reality Check

ARE YOU BEING HELD CAPTIVE IN A STRANGE LAND? Are you being forced to sing a happy tune, as though nothing is wrong? Are you a wounded warrior, a veteran of past organizational battles— one who knows what's going on and who refuses to sing along? Are you being told to act like a model Christian, while not being allowed to call attention to what is being modeled back to you? Does your heart ache when the place where you work or worship is not committed, as you are, to being Christlike in everything it does?

As you weep in the midst of your heartache, what keeps you going? What is deep within your heart, that God has put there, that aches so very much and that you will not allow your tormentors to mock?

Let the Psalmist's lament speak to your heart.[1] He tells of a time of weeping by the rivers of Babylon. He recognizes the tyranny of the tormentors, who demand that the captives sing the joyful songs stored deep within their hearts. He remembers the city of God imprinted upon the hearts of the captives. He responds, "We shall not sing the Lord's song in a strange land!" God, speaking through David and the people of Israel, is confirming what you may also be sensing deep within you: REMEMBER WHO YOU ARE IN THE LORD, AND DO NOT COMPROMISE WHAT HE HAS SHOWN YOU.

One of the most powerful stories I have ever heard about not compromising what God has imprinted upon one's heart is a story that has been retold many times. Perhaps it has lost some accuracy in the details with much retelling, but it is a true story. It was originally told by Billy Kim and took place in North Korea.

The Communist takeover of North Korea was on a village-by-village basis. In one of the villages, the soldiers assembled everyone inside the local church. They found out who the elders of the church were and brought them up to the front. Then they took a picture of Jesus off the wall and ordered the elders to walk one by one past the picture, deny Jesus, and spit on the picture.

When the elders had finished, the soldiers looked over the rest of the villagers and brought a 12-year-old girl up to the front of the church. They told her to pick up the picture of Jesus that had been thrown to the floor and spit on it. She said, "No, I cannot do that after all that Jesus did for me." Then she wiped the spittle off the picture with her skirt, kissed the face of Jesus, handed the picture to her tormentors and said, "You can do with me what you want." The soldiers, obviously shaken, turned to the elders and yelled scornfully, "If you could so easily deny your Jesus, then you'd be no good in the Communist Party!" The elders were ordered to go outside and were then lined up and shot.

Another powerful but less dramatic story of the courage of conviction over compromise is the "stronger than steel" story of Wayne Alderson.[2] In the early 1970s, Wayne was the vice president in charge of operations at Pittron Steel, a steel foundry in Glassport, Pennsylvania. The working conditions of the foundry were abominable: full of noise pollution, air pollution and filth. And they were apprehensible: labor unrest and racial hatred. On the surface, the workers felt betrayed by management's reneging on a promise to make up lost benefits. Underneath, the issue was a matter of dignity and personal respect.

Alderson recognized that the real enemy of labor was not management, per se. Instead, it was an attitude of devaluing people. Inspired by God, he came up with a plan he called Operation Turnaround. It was not just another company promise but a systematic change of the behavior of both rank and file. Operation Turnaround was based on the "Value of the Person" concept, which in turn was based on the biblical virtues of love, dignity and respect.

Operation Turnaround was a great success. It validated Alderson's maxims that (a) productivity must be seen as a byproduct of valuing people, and (b) profits must be seen as accountable to biblical stewardship. In other words, profit must never justify exploitative practices, and profit must itself be governed by the laws of righteousness. The entire company really did turn around. In the twenty-one months of Operation Turnaround's history, reconciliation replaced alienation, and a profit of six million dollars replaced a deficit of six million dollars.

God came to Pittron Steel in a special, tangible way. Wayne Alderson was conducting Bible studies during the lunch hour with the workers all during Operation Turnaround. The studies gradually evolved into a major event every Wednesday, with their own chapel. Workers, and then later managers as well, came together as co-laborers. They began to better understand who God is and that they, as human beings, were equal in His sight.

Pittron Steel began attracting national attention as a successful company. Soon a corporate takeover was in the works, and the new ownership began hinting that Operation Turnaround made them nervous. Wayne knew that his job would be on the line, but he also knew that he would never compromise.

The beginning of the end came with the visit of executives from Bucyrus-Erie, the new owner. Wayne was given full assurance that the visit would not be on a Wednesday, so that there would be no interference with the chapel time. But sure enough, they did come on a Wednesday, and they scheduled a meeting with all the managers during chapel time. Wayne was furious at the betrayal and said curtly that he would be there as soon as the Bible discussion was over. Minutes later he was summoned again. It was an ultimatum. All managers were required to be there. Now.

Against their protestations, Wayne released the other managers to go to the meeting, saying he would join them shortly. Wayne then prayed with the men, and the Lord released the Holy Spirit to guide the discussion that followed. There was fear in the air—fear of returning to the old ways. There was also faith that God would continue to work in their midst. And, as the lunch hour came to a close, there was unity.

Wayne quickly went to the managers' meeting, but it was over. He went home, mulling over the day's events. He had defied authority, postponing a direct order from his superiors. But they had betrayed him, and he didn't want to disappoint the men. What about revenge? He could close the plant. The men would follow him.

Two days later, Wayne flew to Milwaukee to meet the chairman of Bucyrus-Erie and discuss his future. The chairman said that Wayne was one of the most brilliant managers he'd ever seen, but that he had problems with Wayne's management style. The insubordination incident was not the issue, he said, nor was religion, per se, the issue. Chapel on the work site, with managers and workers together, was the issue. He asked Wayne to give up the chapels.

This was the moment of truth. Compromise flitted through Wayne's mind. If he gave up the chapels, at least he would be able to continue to have a positive influence on the workers in other ways. But he remembered God's hand on his own life and all that God had done through the Bible studies. He remembered what God had shown him about the value of the person being God's ideal for the company. God had not given up on him then. Wayne would not give up on God now. He would not compromise. Wayne's response was that no, he would *not* give them up.

Wayne was fired. Or rather, as his wife, Nancy, told him, he was released by God for other ministry. Scripture says that the Lord brings us out in order to lead us in.[3] That has certainly been true for Wayne Alderson. His continuing Value of the Person ministry has taken on new dimensions and directions and has had considerable impact worldwide.

Remembering who you are in Christ and not compromising what He has shown you, actually comprise Phase Two of the recovery process. Phase Two is the pause in the recovery process that keeps hope alive. It is the wellspring, without which recovery is dead.

When you remember your Christian identity and your Christian ideals, you drink the Cup of Blessing. You will be blessed when you are guided by your remembrance of these things. When you refuse to compromise your trust in God, you drink the Cup of Acceptance. This will prepare you for the hard tasks that lie ahead. When everything is in turmoil, and nothing is as it should be, trust in the Lord and He will give you peace.

This chapter is about you and, more precisely, about your calling as a Christian. This is the most fundamental issue for you as a Christian worker. This chapter is also about your organization—the ideal organization that you carry around in your head, which you believe would relieve you of your pain if it existed. The chapter following this one will take up the ideal form of leadership: servant leadership. Both chapters are referred to as biblical reality checks, because each point must be compatible with biblical Christianity.

What Is My Calling?

"I've just lost my job! I'm a Christian, thirty-five years old. It was God's will that I take the job ten years ago, and now I don't have it anymore. That's the job God wanted me to have, and now it's gone. I'm out of God's will. I've been kicked out of the kingdom."

This man was desperate. I didn't know quite what to say. Our conversation was taking place live on a radio talk show, and we had to keep it moving along. But as his story unfolded, it became clear that he was equating his job with his calling. To lose his job, which was his "calling," was to be without a call—to have lost his place in God's kingdom.

So I explained to him that career and calling are not the same thing. We are called to follow Jesus, and He leads us into any number of different jobs. But we are never without a call just because we lose a job. Our calling always remains the same: to follow Jesus.

We prayed, and I moved on to the next person on the line. I have often thought afterward that career-as-calling is a major stumbling block on the road back to wholeness and hope. Whatever happens on the job or to the job itself, however much you may hurt and however much you may agonize over your job, your calling does not change. Your job might change, but your call to follow Jesus never changes.

Most biblical scholars agree that in the New Testament, calling is a technical term for the process of salvation. Many verses can be cited to make the point, and this verse in 1 Corinthians is representative of them: "God, who has called you into fellowship with his Son Jesus Christ our Lord, is faithful."[4] The book of Romans spells it out even further. In it, Paul indicates that within the calling to follow Christ there is also a special setting apart for the gospel:

> Paul, a servant of Jesus Christ, *called to be an apostle*, set apart for the gospel of God which he promised beforehand through his prophets in the holy scriptures, the gospel concerning his Son, who was descended from David according to the flesh and designated Son of God in power according to the Spirit of holiness by his resurrection from the dead, Jesus Christ our Lord, through whom we have received grace and apostleship to bring about the obedience of faith for the sake of his name among all the nations, including yourselves who are *called to belong to Jesus Christ*;
>   To all God's beloved in Rome, who are *called to be saints*:
>   Grace to you and peace from God our Father and the Lord Jesus Christ [emphases mine].[5]

You are as a Christian called into fellowship with Christ, called to belong to Christ and called to be a saint. Paul, however, was also called to be an apostle, a special setting apart for those whose task is specifically to spread the gospel. Pastors and perhaps missionaries can be included in this special calling, but the vast majority of Christians in other jobs are not. The importance of this difference is not that one group is holy and the other is not, that one is sacred and the other is secular, or that one is more special than the other. On the contrary, your calling—every Christian's calling—is a heavenly calling[6] and a holy calling.[7] The important thing to note is that regardless of how one may be set apart, *all* of God's beloved are called to the same thing: to follow Christ.

Perhaps this is confusing to you, further complicated by the verse that in one Bible translation reads, "I therefore, the prisoner of the Lord, beseech you that ye walk worthy of the vocation wherewith ye are called."[8] It sounds like you are being called to a specific vocation—a specific job—doesn't it? In reality, though, "vocation" in this case refers not to making a living but to living a life. Other translations make it more clear: "As a prisoner for the Lord, then, I urge you to live a life worthy of the calling you have received."[9] Continuing on, we read what living "a life worthy of our calling" entails:

> Be completely humble and gentle; be patient, bearing with one another in love. Make every effort to keep the unity of the Spirit through the bond of peace. There is one body and one Spirit— just as you were called to one hope when you were called—one Lord, one faith, one baptism; one God and Father of all, who is over all and through all and in all.[10]

In summary, you and all Christians have the same calling:

- Called into fellowship with Christ
- Called to belong to Christ
- Called to be saints
- Called to live a life worthy of your calling
- Called to one hope in one Lord, who is over all and through all and in all.

You are called to live up to your name: Christian, or follower of Christ. You are to be a disciple of the Christ who emptied Himself and took the form of a servant. You are to follow Him, serving others, as your calling, whatever your job may be or whatever your job situation may be like. Your hope is in Christ, not in your career. You may lose your career, but you cannot lose your calling. You are a Christian!

WHAT IS THE IDEAL ORGANIZATION?

Scripture does not answer this question directly, as it does "What is my calling?" and "What is servant leadership?" I will therefore paint a picture of the ideal organization with broad strokes, one that is nevertheless compatible with biblical Christianity. You will have to fill in the details yourself, as they relate to your particular organization.

Thinking idealistically is important. It is important so that you can keep your bearings amidst the unjust and uncaring things that may be happening where you work. It is important so that you can give truthful and loving witness to those around you. And finally, it is important so that you can hold yourself and your leader(s) accountable to standards that are pleasing to God.

Just about everybody, I would imagine, has some ideas about what would make things better. Most ideas, I would speculate further, involve what could be taken away to make things better. What could you get rid of? Or whom? What policy or procedure could you get rid of? What person or group of people could you get rid of? It would be perfect, wouldn't it, if you didn't have that stupid policy or if you could just fire old so-and-so? Things would be good if you could only get rid of the bad.

Scripture has a different view. It's true that we are told to correct those who do wrong and dissociate from those who cause division—to remove the bad. But we are also encouraged to add something good. This is illustrated by the Old Testament story of Elisha and the kettle:

When Elisha returned to Gilgal, there was a famine in the land. As the sons of the prophets were sitting before him, he said to his servant, "Put on the big kettle, and boil stew for the sons of the prophets." So one of them went out to the field to gather herbs. He found a wild vine from which he gathered his lap full of wild gourds. He cut up the herbs into the kettle, not knowing what they were. Then he poured it out for the men to eat. But when they ate of the herbs, they cried out, "There is death in the kettle, O man of God!"; for they could not eat it. He said, "Bring here some flour," and when he had thrown it into the kettle, he said, "Pour it out for the people, that they may eat." And there was nothing harmful in the kettle.[11]

When there is death in the kettle—neurosis, addiction, spiritual abuse—we should not always look only at taking out the bad stuff. We can also heal our organizational ills by what we add, not just by what we remove.

I often ask the workers in Christian organizations which I do consulting with to describe their ideal organization. What would they add to their present organization to make it ideal? Here is one of their replies:

We would work in teams. We would have leaders who believe in us and encourage us to do things we didn't know we could do. We would have a wonderful feeling of accomplishment. There would be good communication between leadership and workers. Everyone at all levels would serve one another for the common good rather than compete with one another to get ahead at someone else's expense.

What I would add, first and foremost, would be to make all jobs fulfilling, with opportunities to be creative and take responsibility. Then I would add a communication system where everyone has input into decisions that will affect them before the decisions are made. Third, I would add procedures that allow people to voice concerns without being viewed as troublemakers and that provide equity rather than special perks for the haves and nothing for the have-nots.

This Christian worker's response has within it the two most common elements of the ideal Christian organization, as reported to me by dozens of workers in a wide variety of Christian organizations. They are *empowerment*, which we will consider next, and *servant leadership*, which we will take up in the following chapter.

Empowerment

The concept of empowerment has exploded into the workplace consciousness. There are three principles of empowerment that I would like to consider. They are (a) work must have a *worthwhile purpose*, (b) work must involve *meaningful participation*, and (c) work must foster *personal responsibility*.

The first principle points out that, at the very least, you want to be able to say that your work has a worthwhile purpose. The workers I have talked with are unanimous in saying that their work must have a purpose—that it must be about something worthwhile. Some say that their work must have integrity of purpose. Others maintain that their work must make a definite contribution to the organization and to other people. Still others add that their work needs to directly serve others.

The second principle of empowerment requires that work also be based on meaningful participation. The examples of participation of employees, participation of the laity and participative management have been around for a long time. However, they are generally present only in principle, not in practice. Most people think that participation is a great idea, but most organizations either don't allow it, or don't allow it to be truly meaningful. Meaningful participation requires that workers, at least to some degree, have input into the planning process, decision-making process and problem-solving process. How often have you seen that in Christian—or non-Christian—organizations?

It has been said that participation is a moral obligation.[12] It is claimed that highly nonparticipative jobs can cause psychological impairment and even physical harm over the long haul. It is also claimed, on the other hand, that participative jobs can definitely improve both psychological and physical health. Therefore, if it is wrong to harm others psychologically and physically, then participation is a moral issue. The claim is controversial, but the secular literature has picked it up and argued that participation in terms of far-ranging input throughout the organizational structure is almost an imperative.

In contrast, the Christian literature has not made participation a moral issue. If people in the church made it a moral issue, however, perhaps more Christian organizations would wholeheartedly implement the principle of meaningful participation. The church, in my opinion, should take the lead in this area. But Christian organizations are unfortunately just like secular organizations, by and large paying only lip service to it. "In practice, participative management is frequently a rhetoric of management that protects the seat of control and power at the top. Interestingly enough, we have found those groups, like the church, that are supposedly 'more moral' are also frequently very deceptive about participative management."[13] We do not walk the talk. That is a sad commentary indeed.

When an organization is deficient and deceptive in providing opportunities for participation, individuals within the organization are wounded not only psychologically and physically, but also spiritually. In the extreme case, as in a cult, where a single leader has the vision that everyone must follow and is supposedly the exclusive conduit through whom God addresses the people, the individual is stunted spiritually. People in such organizations do not expect to meet God in Scripture, so they do not read to learn. The leader, it is assumed, will teach what is in Scripture.

In abusive organizations such as this, individual Christians lose their ability to discern and heed the promptings of the Holy Spirit. They rely on the leadership to hear God's voice for them. Without ears to hear for themselves the voice of God, they no longer have the authority of God to speak the word of God, either to themselves or to others. It is likely that they will lose their sense of calling, and that the leadership and the organization itself will lose the word of correction that God intended for them to hear. When workers do not participate in the discernment process, everybody loses.

The third principle of empowerment in the workplace concerns personal responsibility. Empowering work fosters personal responsibility at two levels: first, in creating a shared corporate vision and, second, in being responsible for personal survival. At the shared-vision level, it means that the vision for the future of the organization is not just figured out at the top and carried out at the bottom. In other words, the vision is not just based on compliance, but rather on commitment; not just on obligation, but on ownership.

In most organizations, the corporate vision is simply announced from on high. Many churches, for example, hire a pastor with a vision, or the board of elders goes off on a retreat to write its vision statement. Then they try to get the congregation to "buy into" the vision. They "sell" it. At best they will get compliance, not real commitment. People will go along, drone-like, with the leadership's dream, but they will not own it. The vision is not their vision. They only "bought" it. They did not help create it.

Shared vision is a common identity that incorporates personal visions. Empowering organizations encourage individual members to develop their own visions. Empowering organizations also enroll every member at every level of the organization into a process of sharing their personal visions. This can be an open-ended process of developing a corporate vision from scratch, with no initial version to use as a basis for discussion. Or, more commonly, the process can be centered around the vision of one person. Quite often the leader fills the role of providing the initial vision, then encourages a process of interaction and dialogue. The leader repeats his or her vision, while everyone adds to it, refines it and makes it come alive. In the end, they can all say, "The final vision truly is *our* vision."

The second level of taking personal responsibility occurs at the level of personal survival. Empowering organizations do not make survival political. Rather, they simply put personal survival into the individual's own hands. They create a climate where there is no one to blame but oneself. The clearest example is in the area of performance. People are rewarded for their competence, not their machinations and manipulations to get ahead. Evaluation is based on performance, not on politics or personality.

Another example is in the area of protection. Empowering organizations do not make personal survival dependent on being protected by or from others. People are encouraged to take initiative, work up to their capabilities, offer constructive solutions, and admit their mistakes and learn from them. They are discouraged from letting others do for them what they can do for themselves and from continually finding fault and blaming others for their own failures.

Finding fault and blaming are perverted forms of dependency. They are the framework of one's fortress of protection against the future. Faultfinders and blamers are often people who politicize and personalize everything that happens to go the least bit sideways. Because they are so anxious about the future, they simply wait until someone else does something before they will act. Then if it's done wrong or not done at all, it's someone else's fault. Their dependence on someone else to be the fall guy protects them against doing something wrong themselves.

These same people also seek protection from being victimized by someone else unintentionally doing something wrong. So they again wait to see what someone else does before taking any action themselves. Has this happened to you? Have you been hurt by others, because they didn't seem to know what they were doing? And are you just waiting to see if you will become a victim again before you take any action yourself? If so, one of your wounds is helplessness. And I may have a solution.

Try looking at your situation this way. Let's say this other person is your boss or pastor. You are blaming him or her for apparent incompetence in an area that inconveniences you, frustrates you or causes you to fail. Consider this question: Can your life go on anyway, because this is not a category of abuse that affects everything else you do? What if your boss (pastor) is doing all he or she can? Maybe it's not just the appearance of incompetence—

maybe it *is* incompetence. Also, consider another question: Can you forgive rather than blame him or her for that? Sure, you're disappointed and angry because your boss (pastor) does not measure up to what a leader should be. But can you accept that he or she may have done as well as he or she can, and can you stop waiting and watching for him or her to mess up again? Can you forgive and get on with your life?

The lesson here is that dependence on being protected by and from others holds us back. Yes, it lets us off the hook and keeps us out of harm's way. But it also keeps us helpless. Helplessness is a wound, and it is not Christ's way. Christ alone is our protection, and He alone is our future. Jesus said that He is the way and the truth (our protection) and the life (our future).[14]

The story of Elisha and the kettle tells us to add something good. What can the organization add for the empowerment of its workers? Wayne Alderson's Value of the Person concept, based on the biblical virtues of love, dignity and respect, is a good place to start. The following summary should also help you as you put together your thoughts on the ideal organization. It incorporates some of the ideas already mentioned and also includes ideas from a variety of other sources:[15]

1. *Meaning.* What workers and leaders do is genuinely needed and faithfully expresses biblical values.
2. *Mastery.* Workers and leaders continually clarify and deepen the meaning they attach to their work/ministry by learning as much as they can about what they do. They continuously strive for excellence and faithfully develop their God-given giftedness.
3. *Integrity.* Workers and leaders put into words what they see happening and speak the truth in love. They say what they mean and mean what they say, and share information

accurately and completely. They make only those promises they can keep, and admit to their mistakes.

4. *Service.* Workers and leaders genuinely contribute to the organization and its mission. They promote the welfare of others, and they are servants to one another.

5. *Team-building.* Workers and leaders dialogue together across management/nonmanagement and clergy/laity lines. This dialogue aids discernment and forms plans of action for them as a community of colaborers/believers.

6. *Shared vision.* Workers and leaders covenant with one another for their future together. In the Christian organization, workers and leaders covenant with one another to further God's kingdom as He discloses needs and guides and provides for proper response.

7. *Worldview thinking.* Workers and leaders apply their fundamental, biblically compatible values and beliefs to everything that they do. In the Christian organization, workers and leaders utilize biblical principles in their approach to every opportunity and every obstacle that they encounter and also in their critique of every action that they take.

For Christian workers who have not been empowered and have been wounded instead, and for Christian organizations that have wavered from the ideal, let this be your remembrance:

As you have therefore received Christ, (even) Jesus the Lord, (so) walk (regulate your lives and conduct yourselves) in union with *and* conformity to Him.

Have the roots (of your being) firmly *and* deeply planted (in Him, fixed and founded in Him), being continually built up in Him, becoming increasingly more confirmed *and* established in the faith, just as you were taught, and abounding *and* overflowing in it with thanksgiving.[16]

Doing a Biblical
Reality Check

PART II

T HE IDEAL FORM OF LEADERSHIP in most, if not all, organizations is
servant leadership. At the core of servant leadership is the
biblical concept of servanthood. Servanthood is also central to
biblical guidelines for relating to one another. Therefore, this
chapter is not just about leaders. It is about everyone in the
organization.

I love what Paul says: "I am not bound to obey anyone just
because he pays my salary; yet I have freely and happily become a
servant of any and all."[1] You have been set free from bondage to a
neurotic employer, an addictive organization or a spiritually abusive
pastor. You are free in Christ, yet you are bound by love to serve
others: "For you were called to freedom, brethren; only do not use
your freedom as an opportunity for the flesh, but through love be
servants of one another."[2]

As a wounded worker, you are called out of bondage to freedom
in Christ. And in that freedom is the opportunity to serve others
with the love of Christ. Leaders are also called to freedom in Christ
to serve others with the love of Christ. Workers and leaders alike,

whether wounded or not, and at every level of the organization, are called to the same thing. All are called to be servants of one another—to servanthood—which is the essence of servant leadership.

WHAT IS SERVANT LEADERSHIP?

We have already added empowerment to Elisha's kettle, in chapter 6. Now we must add servant leadership to the kettle. The ingredients of servanthood are listed in the Old Testament, and the recipe is so good that it was copied in the New Testament. In the Book of Isaiah, we read:

> See my servant, whom I uphold; my Chosen One, in whom I delight. I have put my Spirit upon him; he will reveal justice to the nations of the world. He will be gentle—he will not shout nor quarrel in the streets. He will not break the bruised reed, nor quench the dimly burning flame. He will encourage the fainthearted, those tempted to despair. He will see full justice given to all who have been wronged.[3]

In the New Testament, Matthew repeats the entire paragraph from Isaiah and shows the fulfillment of the prophecy in Jesus Christ.[4] So, being a servant is being like Jesus, and following Isaiah's recipe. There are four ingredients listed. I would like to propose four phrases that I believe accurately represent them and suggest a description for each phase that correctly reflects the thinking of various biblical scholars.

According to Scripture, servanthood involves (a) *being gentle*—being humble, kind and considerate, not contentious or disrespectful. It involves (b) *bearing with*—patiently enduring, with affectionate regard, those who are weak or disheartened. It involves (c) *building up*—strengthening those who are timid or discouraged. And it involves (d) *bringing justice*—helping those who have been injured or dishonored.

I would add one more, because Scripture records that Jesus was a suffering servant, as He endured the indignity and pain of the cross on our behalf. Therefore, servanthood also involves (e) *blessing others*—sacrificing self-interest for the good of others, for those who are without hope and direction. Selfishness or self-interest is just the opposite of servanthood, and the prophet Jeremiah has a word for it: "Every one from the least . . . to the greatest is guilty of unjust gain; every one from the prophet to the priest practices deceit. Hence they have healed the wound of my people slightly, saying, 'Peace, peace,' when there is no peace."[5]

The word that Jeremiah uses for self-interest is *deceit*. Deceit, in the biblical context, is the seeking of one's own advancement rather than the welfare of other people. Deceit is the agent of defilement of Christian (and non-Christian) organizations. The people cry out for a say in decisions that affect them and weep tears of powerlessness and of being abused. Christians struggle with the decision of whether to take another Christian to court to obtain at least a semblance of justice. Workers are treated with disrespect, they are disheartened and discouraged, and they suffer dishonor and are directionless. The self-interested leader can heal these wounds only slightly, just as Jeremiah says. And the leader who will not tell the truth because it won't look good, and who proclaims, "Peace, peace," when there is no peace, just makes matters worse.

Being Gentle and Bearing with

Most people desire to work in a place where everyone is humble, kind and considerate and not contentious or disrespectful. They want leadership that will patiently endure, with affectionate regard, those who are weak or disheartened. Many of those in leadership positions, however, will argue that business can't afford utopias. There is too much work to be done, and all that warm fuzzy stuff would be totally counterproductive. Same thing in the church and parachurch. Personal needs, they say (either directly or indirectly) must be sacrificed for the ministry and for the furtherance of the Lord's work.

One reason biblical principles of servanthood are not the norm in Christian organizations in particular is the fundamental conflict between serving those inside and serving those outside the organization. In business and parachurch organizations, the emphasis is usually on caring for the customer. In the church, the emphasis is often on ministering to the unchurched (or prechurched). These are given top priority. The employees and church members, on the other hand, often feel that their needs are not being met and that they are not cared for. They feel that they are not treated as considerately or respected as much as those outside the organization. As an employee of a parachurch ministry put it: "I would like to see us model some of the same principles that our ministry is all about right here within the walls of our own organization. It's an integrity issue for me. We apply the Bible to our donors and the people we serve, but if we work here, we don't get treated that way."

This is in fact an *integrity* issue. It is a matter of deceit. When we appear one way on the outside and live differently on the inside, it is almost being Christian in name only. This is another form of the deceit referred to by the prophet Jeremiah. It is integrity in the head but not in the heart.

If we are to be servants of one another, we will do well to pattern ourselves after David when he was at his best. In the Psalms, we read that David served as a leader or shepherded according to the integrity of his heart. Shepherding involved his entire being and was inspired from the depth of his being. Everything he did was cut from the same piece of cloth and represented "his best instincts."[6] Well, just about everything.

Too many today—leaders and workers alike—act as David sometimes did, according to "their worst instincts." They do whatever will help them survive rather than what is right. Too many will say whatever they think you want to hear. Too many will not tell the truth. They will not or cannot deal honestly with information in an accurate, complete and upright fashion. This problem really has two parts to it: *collecting* information and *communicating* information.

First, collecting information is a problem for the person who already has his or her mind made up ("Don't confuse me with the facts") and who impulsively makes decisions before knowing all the facts. This person should beware: "The way of the foolish is right in his own eyes, but the wise listens to advice,"[7] and "What a shame—yes, how stupid!—to decide before knowing the facts!"[8]

Deciding before knowing the facts makes it very difficult, for example, to bear with and act redemptively toward someone who seems to have done something wrong. Sometimes a member of the organization's constituency or one of its customers registers a complaint about an employee. When that happens, it is imperative to collect accurate and complete information: "Surely the Law does not allow us to pass judgment on a man without giving him a hearing and discovering what he is about?"[9] Discovering what he or she is about—that is what everyone deserves. Bearing with those who are accused is essentially discovering what they are about—letting them tell their story, understanding their own experience of what happened, and interacting with their full range of thoughts and feelings about what has happened and what should happen next.

This is so obvious and the only decent thing to do, and yet it routinely does not occur, especially in those organizations that are struggling for survival. They take every powerful constituent's complaint, particularly if it is a doctrinal issue, extremely seriously and often take disciplinary action before taking the time to give the accused a hearing. They have to set an example, limit the damage and put it behind them, they say. How sad and how unbiblical to put financial security ahead of integrity.

The second part of dealing honestly with information is communicating it. Again, this can be a problem for anyone within the organization but especially for leaders who like to present different sides to different people, to tell a different story depending on who is listening. It may simply involve illuminating one side of an issue to one group and a different side of the same issue to another group, and there may be no conflict between the two stories. But it may also involve leaving out a little bit of information here and exaggerating a little bit there. It is pretty obvious how political and self-serving this can become. And it can escalate. For someone who has maneuvered to control information flow and who is well-practiced at impression management, there can be no greater challenge to his or her integrity.

Scripture could not be any more clear when it tells us to set forth the facts truthfully—plainly, without deception or distortion.[10] Don't lie.

Becoming a servant of any and all, means being gentle and bearing with. In a word, being *benevolent*. Benevolence is the straightforward expression of kindness and tolerance that the apostle Paul describes so well: "The Lord's servant must not be a man of strife: he must be kind to all, ready and able to teach: he must be tolerant and have the ability gently to correct those who oppose his message."[11]

I am sad to say that there are Christian organizations, churches included, where there is very little tolerance or bearing with. Take, for instance, the pastor who is threatened by those who have gifts that he does not possess. He is threatened because in his mind he must be the best at everything, so all other persons and gifts must be subordinated to him. But that certainly is not the picture of what a pastor—a servant—should be. His job is to recognize and encourage others' giftedness and accommodate and help in the development of their gifts. In fact, this will most likely have to be done at some sacrifice of personal comfort because of the tension caused by change in the status quo.

Benevolence is bearing *with*. It is not bearing *down*. It is not being contentiously protective of one's position. It is not firing people for "insubordination" when they disagree with a decision or complain about the quality of leadership, or just because their competence challenges the one who's in charge.

Benevolence is redemptive discipline, whereby an employee who is not cutting it is worked with, so that he or she can become a better person, worker and Christian. The employee is not treated as a problem to be gotten rid of as soon as possible. Redemptive discipline is pleasing to God. He cannot be pleased when, as so often happens in Christian organizations, a person is unredemptively disciplined and let go, and then goes to work for another Christian organization. Then we smugly congratulate ourselves because we think we are now a stronger organization, and everything is okay because the person got another job. God is interested primarily in His kingdom, which includes all Christian organizations, not just our precious little kingdom. We may be better off, but the kingdom of God is not.

In Paul's words, the Lord's servants are to be ready and able first and foremost to teach rather than terminate, and to gently correct rather than condemn the ones who disagree with their message and who perhaps even oppose them.

Finally, being servants to one another by being gentle and bearing with one another involves *caring for* one another. The prophet Ezekiel warns us to do no less:

> The word of the Lord came to me: Son of man, prophesy against the shepherds of Israel. Prophesy; say to them, Thus says the Lord God to the shepherds: Ah! You shepherds of Israel, who have been tending yourselves; should not shepherds tend the sheep? . . . The weak you have not strengthened; nor have you healed the sick or bound up the wounded; nor have you brought back the straying or sought after the lost; only with force and with rigor have you ruled over them.[12]

The Lord is calling the shepherds of Israel, and all Christians in a leadership capacity, to tend the sheep, not rule them with force and malevolence. Leaders are to care for the weak, sick and wounded, bringing back those who stray and seeking after those who are lost. It can be reasonably assumed, therefore, that they must care for those who cannot continue at the same level of performance or at the same job due to age or injury. They must care for those who have violated a policy or procedure of the organization and even those who have turned against them and their way of doing things.

What does *caring for* mean in these cases? It means providing new opportunities for those with diminished capabilities, forgiving and redemptively disciplining those who have made a mistake, and reasoning together with those who have basic differences of opinion. Caring for is tending, bringing back or seeking after—whatever is needed in order to be a good shepherd.

A prime test for how we care for one another in any organization is how we treat those who "stay with the baggage": "The share of him who stays with the baggage shall be equal to the share of him who marches to battle."[13]   This verse tells us to look closely at those who have the least—the least power, the least visibility, the least responsibility. The quickest way to spot these folks is to check out the salary structure of the organization.

Do the highest and lowest salaries reflect Paul's admonition that the one who gathers much does not have too much, and the one who gathers little does not have too little?[14]   Does the president get a higher annual percentage increase in salary than the lowest-paid employee?   And what about when hard times hit?   Are employees being laid off while executives are getting pay raises? Why doesn't the belt-tightening start at the top?

Building Up

Do you work at a place where everything seems to be geared toward building up a profit?   Do you worship at a church where primary emphasis is put on building up attendance? Or building a building?   How many Christian or non-Christian organizations can you name where building up people is at least as important as any of these? In my experience, building up people too often takes a back seat.   When push comes to shove, the workers and the worshipers have to give way.

Give way to what?   Corporate profit?   Constituency pressure? Doctrinal purity?   There are perhaps dozens of answers to the question.   But the important issue here is who or what decides. Who or what decides that a seminary student, trusted for his sincerity, integrity and biblical concerns, who speaks out against the Vietnam War, will be dismissed from school because the seminary's financial needs require it? Who or what decides that a mature Christian woman cannot be Sunday school superintendent because she doesn't, in her own mocking words, "shave in the morning"? "Authority" decides.

My concern is not so much with the act of decision making as it is with the attitude of the decision maker. The attitude that one has about authority is at the very heart of his or her ability to be a servant to others. One Christian who perhaps understood this best, and who personally experienced the power of authority to either build up or break down, was Dietrich Bonhoeffer. Beginning in 1933 with his first run-in with the German leadership, and continuing with his refusal to cooperate with the Nazi government and with his incarceration in Gestapo prisons, authority defined Bonhoeffer's life. It even defined his death: He was executed in 1945 by special order of Heinrich Himmler. But Bonhoeffer also defined authority and enriched our understanding of it immensely.

Genuine authority, according to Bonhoeffer, is a ministry. It exists in a life of servanthood. We don't usually think of it in that way but rather more as an end unto itself. Genuine authority is a means to the end of ministry, of service to others. According to Bonhoeffer, genuine authority "is to be found only where the ministry of hearing, helping, bearing, and proclaiming is carried out."[15] Genuine authority lies in listening "with the ears of God that we may speak the Word of God."[16] It lies in not contradicting our sincerity by our own lack of helpfulness. It lies in conveying a spirit of bearing with, not of impatience and the desire to force acceptance. Bonhoeffer cuts to the quick:

> The desire we so often hear expressed today for "episcopal figures," "priestly men," "authoritative personalities" springs frequently enough from a spiritually sick need for the admiration of men, for the establishment of visible human authority, because the genuine authority of service appears to be so unimpressive. There is nothing that so sharply contradicts such a desire as the New Testament itself in its description of a bishop (I Tim. 3:1 ff.). One finds there nothing whatsoever with respect to worldly charm and the brilliant attributes of a spiritual personality. The bishop is the simple, faithful man, sound in faith and life, who rightly discharges his duties to the Church. His authority lies in the exercise of his ministry. In the man himself there is nothing to admire.[17]

134 / CHAPTER SEVEN

That is not the usual view of authority. Authority is usually seen as a personal attribute or as inherent in a given office or position. Thus, leaders are said to "have" authority over others by virtue of their office or the position they occupy. If a person wants to be a servant leader, however, which is an entirely different concept, authority must be based on legitimized power. It must be seen as given by those over whom it is exercised.[18] In other words, the servant leader is more likely to be true to his or her calling if authority is not assumed, but earned. It must be granted, not grasped.

Authority can be easily abused when it is not seen in this way. When authority is automatic, or an inherent right, and not contingent or dependent upon the response of those who are affected by it, there is nothing in its exercise that in and of itself will prevent abuse. Authority cannot be self-contained: an end unto itself. Something must be added, and that something is service to others. Service to others protects authority against itself.

As Bonhoeffer says, genuine authority lies in the exercise of ministry. It is a consequence of ministry, not a precondition for ministry. Yet neurotic, addictive and spiritually abusive organizations all keep building their own "field of dreams." They keep saying, "If we build it, God will come. Tell people they must sacrifice their own needs for the good of the organization. Establish a clear line of authority. Don't let anyone get out of line. And God will come, and ministry will happen."

I say, "No. God has *already* built it. *We* must come. It is already there, and we must make it our own. It is Jesus' example of servanthood, that is the true basis for ministry." The choice is clear: authority as an end unto itself or authority in the exercise of ministry.

AUTHORITY AS AN END UNTO ITSELF

1. *Business-ministry conflict*—expecting people in the organization to sacrifice their own needs for the good of the business or for ministry to people outside the organization.

2. *Bearing down*—promoting compliance and protection of the leader's position.
3. *Punitive*—taking immediate disciplinary action to make an example of those who go against the grain.
4. *Ruling*—focusing on authority and obedience to authority.
5. *Automatic*—assuming that authority is the inherent right of the leader, independent of what followers might think.

AUTHORITY IN THE EXERCISE OF MINISTRY

1. *Business-ministry convergence*—building up people in the organization as well as building up the business or ministry to people outside the organization.
2. *Bearing with*—patiently encouraging the expression of others' giftedness, with affectionate regard and integrity of heart.
3. *Redemptive*—being ready and able to teach, tolerant and redemptive, gently correcting and discovering what the person is about before passing judgment.
4. *Caring for*—focusing on trust, respect, tending, bringing back and seeking after as the context for the expression of authority.
5. *Contingent*—recognizing that genuine authority is earned and that it is authenticated by the exercise of ministry.

Service to others protects authority against itself, and so does accountability. We hear a lot of talk about accountability these days. What it usually involves is being answerable to superiors and peers. We tend to think that we are completely covered and totally accountable if we answer to people above us who give directions for what we do and to people alongside us who give opinions about how we do it.

There is a certain amount of accountability in one-way, bottom-up accountability with superiors and a certain amount in the mutual, give-and-take accountability among peers. But I do not believe it is totally complete until those who are at the lower levels of responsibility or stations in life are included. We will not be truly accountable until those who receive our services and our orders are allowed to give feedback about how well we do what we do. They are the ones who really know the quality of our service and who grant us the authority to be their servants. I believe that this type of *mutual accountability* is an essential part of the practice of servanthood.

Being answerable to subordinates as well as superiors and peers is difficult for many to accept. Consider Carl Novotny, president of New Church Network Ministries, to accept (fictitious names, factual observations). It is very difficult for him to be vulnerable to the opinion and critique of others, especially if they are employees. Being answerable to bosses and board members, yes, but answerable to employees? This is, for Novotny, going too far. He basically serves himself and his career through impression management and control of information. He merely pays lip service to the concerns of his subordinates, and he makes sure they go no further.

One of the largest obstacles to mutual accountability at NCNM is President Novotny's control of communication with the board of directors. This gatekeeping function, whereby the board receives only the information that Novotny wants it to receive, is very common in Christian as well as in non-Christian organizations. We need to be asking some very hard questions in this area. How can a board accurately evaluate the performance of a leader if the only information it has to work with is provided by the leader who is being evaluated? Even if the leader attempts to present an upset employee's or church member's experience to the board on his or her behalf, it will be done from the leader's perspective. The board is forced to deal with information that is frequently distorted or deficient at least in part. These imperfections are perhaps not always by design, but they are certainly to be expected, given the contrast between firsthand reports on one's own performance and secondhand reports on others' thoughts and behaviors.

The real rub at NCNM has come when an employee has had a legitimate complaint concerning President Novotny and has had to utilize the chain of command in voicing that complaint. One time an employee tried to expose a serious mistake the president had made in an area in which the employee had firsthand knowledge. She spoke to her supervisor and then to the president directly. Novotny's response was to tell everyone that she was disenchanted with NCNM and actually desired to leave. According to Novotny, "She's been telling others about this who have come to me about it, and I was able to set them straight. She's causing a lot of trouble. She's just unhappy working here." Accurate information will never reach the board, and President Novotny will guarantee it.

Are you an aggrieved employee or an agitated member of a church, and the board does not know what is going on? Are you saying to yourself that the board should know such and such, but there just is no way to let them know? Have you seriously considered writing a letter to the board? What an unfortunate misuse of creative energy that would be, energy that could be used so much more productively if lines of communication were not obstructed. What a joy it would be to know that the board has direct access to information at all levels of the organization. What a joy to know that everybody is accountable, regardless of his or her station in life.

Many organizations do not want mutual accountability between superiors and subordinates. They want accountability, of course, but without the mutual part. They want strict accountability to superiors so that no one will get out of line. They want "harmony," or at least the appearance of it.

One of the central myths of organizational folklore is that harmony is always desirable. In fact, the driving force behind the unfair treatment of people in organizations is quite often an unyielding desire for harmony. The leadership of dysfunctional and stagnant organizations typically will do almost anything to preserve at least the illusion of harmony. Let anyone with a difference of opinion or a prophetic call for change speak out, and he or she will be silenced. We therefore need to ask another hard question:

Why must a person who has an honest difference of opinion with the organizational powers be silenced or domesticated or driven out so that the public can continue to believe—falsely—

that organizational life is without strife? And yet organizations
continue to assume the most contrived postures in order to
maintain the illusion of harmony—postures such as lying to the
public.

Our inability to transcend the dangerous notion that we don't
wash our dirty linen in public verges on the schizophrenic. It
implies not only that dissent is bad but that our . . . institutions
. . . are made up not of human beings but of saints who never
engage in such vulgar and offensive activities. Thus, [each
institution] strives to be regarded as a hallowed shrine where
. . . "the meanest lust for power can be sanctified and the dullest
wit greeted with reverential awe."[19]

The "hallowed shrine" is a dangerous place to work. Life
without strife—the Bible doesn't promise that. And lying to the
public and lusting for power—that is not God's provision for *any*
organization, including the Christian organization seeking to be
Christ-centered in all that it does.

The ideal organization provides an atmosphere not just of the
appearance of harmony but of *true harmony*. Harmony is like
peace—the latter is not just the absence of war, and the former is
not just the absence of dissent. True harmony makes room for and
arises out of honest differences of opinion and grows when we
speak the truth in love and reason together.

True harmony, ultimately, is true unity: being one in the Spirit
and having oneness in spirit. However, as true harmony contrasts
with the illusion of harmony, unity contrasts with its pretender:
unanimity. We can learn a lot about an organization by comparing
unity and unanimity:[20]

UNITY	UNANIMITY
• An internal quality that can only be profoundly experienced	• An external quality that can be measured, monitored and enforced
• The primary goal is oneness in spirit	• The primary goal is correct behavior

Christian organizations, particularly those in the Evangelical subculture, tend toward unanimity, with orthodoxies of belief and behavior and even of vocabulary. Spiritual jargon easily takes the place of real talk, so real feelings are denied and real questions are discouraged. The following says it beautifully:

> Phony questions, however, where the answer is known by all, are part of a pleasurable ritual. They are asked and answered in a wonderful, nonthreatening confirmation of "group think." The leader voices the supposed objections of nonbelievers—the dreaded secular humanists, for example—then neatly demolishes them. The Christian movie allows twenty minutes or so of rebellion and "questioning God" on the part of its young protagonist, to be followed, as surely as day follows night, by twenty minutes of finding the way back to God and a happy ending. The audience has the thrill of the chase with none of the threat, and goes away satisfied.[21]

Dying organizations are being killed by unanimity and uniformity, by compliance and conformity. They are being barely kept alive by their appearances and by their satisfactions from "the thrill of the chase with none of the threat."

Dynamic, living organizations are fueled by unity and commitment. They thrive on true harmony and the freedom of individuals to embrace the corporate agenda in their own way relative to their own giftedness. They live by faith, not fear, and for the glory of God—not for the glory of their human inclinations.

Bringing Justice

Two great types of servant have had lasting influence on human organizations throughout history. As depicted in the Bible, the two types of servant are the priest and the prophet. As unto the Lord, the priest has always cared for the wounded and tended the flock. Equally as unto the Lord, the prophet has cried out for the wounded and brought justice to the oppressed. These priestly qualities are the servant qualities of being gentle, bearing with and building up. And, of course, the prophetic qualities include the servant quality of bringing justice.

In short, bringing justice is a prophetic ministry. We will need to understand the way of the prophet in order to understand this aspect of servanthood. Accordingly, we will consider two of the primary concerns of prophetic ministry: *identification with the oppressed* and *provision for the poor.*

Identification with the oppressed begins with the recognition of one's own experience of being under oppression. Are you aware of such a time? Do you feel oppressed in your present circumstance? Has it perhaps been so intense that you have not yet been able to put words to it? Are you being oppressed, but you're too numb to complain? Perhaps your organization has what has been called a "management mentality" that is actually numbing your consciousness. Consider the following questions:[22]

1. Does it seem that there are no mysteries, only problems to be solved?
2. Is emphasis primarily on cost-accounting?
3. Does the leadership almost make a religion out of its devotion to optimism?
4. Is everyone looking out only for himself or herself?
5. Is there interest only in people's behavior, which can be managed, and not in what they experience?

The overall effect of the management mentality is to close people off from the conscious awareness of their own experience. Let's look again at the five questions you just answered. Taking them in order, you will be able to see how you may have ended up numbed to your pain. First, the belief that all mysteries are problems to be solved overshadows the promise of personal *faith* as a resource. For example, in a budget crisis where the cause is too complex to fully comprehend, immediate across-the-board cost-cutting is given priority over prayer. Similarly, regardless of the circumstances, so-called objective cost-accounting procedures negate any subjective *feelings* about including prayer in routine business decisions.

Third, optimism, or manipulation of reality by putting on a happy face, substitutes for real *hope.* Fourth, individualism, or promotion of a competitive culture of everyone for himself or herself, nullifies *compassion* for others. And fifth, behaviorism, or control of behavior through denial of personal experience, destroys personal *meaningfulness*.

So, when the operating procedures of organizations with a management mentality disclaim personal faith and feelings and discard hope, compassion and meaningfulness, people become numb to what they are personally experiencing. Becoming numb is about the only way to cope with violation that is so deep and so painful.

What would you like your organization to do to make things better? The ideal, prophetic way is first of all "mobilizing people to their real restless grief."[23] In other words, the leadership of your organization should help people bring their hurt out into the light of day. This can be done by making it safe to self-disclose and by creating forums for people to share their grievances without fear of retribution. By allowing groups of people to interact with one another, some will more readily than others cry out in testimony to their own deep anguish and sorrowful lament. This will articulate the grief of those who hold back and encourage them to join in the expression of their pain, which has been covered over for so long.

Crying out together that things are not right is precisely what most, if not all, organizations try to prevent. Organizations live by their capacity "to still the groans and to go on with business as usual as though none were hurting and there were no groans."[24] They do not have communication channels that allow them to really listen, and when they do hear they are indifferent in their response or coldly silent. As long as they "can keep the pretense alive that things are all right, there will be no real grieving and no serious criticism."[25]

Grieving—the "visceral announcement that things are not right"—is, I must point out, the ultimate form of criticism.[26] This is very important yet is not a widely recognized fact. Grieving shatters immune optimism; anger, indignation and argument do not. They just cause greater distancing by creating adversarial relationships. Grieving, on the other hand, signals loudly and clearly that the managed reality is not being accepted. A new reality is being sought, and grieving is the strongest way in which that message can be communicated.

For those in a Christian organization whose numbness has been replaced by awareness that the old reality is psychologically and spiritually oppressive, the organization must find ways to energize hope for a radically new reality. It must give up old realities and sing a new song of hope. It must find new ways to tell everyone in the organization that there is hope for the future.

For example, could a personnel policy be adopted that requires hearing and discovering what a person is about before judgment is passed? What about making redemptive discipline a corporate policy? What about establishing a reward structure that allows those who "stay with the baggage" an equal share? Perhaps a mutual accountability structure could be set up whereby performance evaluations are done in both directions, up and down the hierarchy. Perhaps the board could work on the problem of gatekeeping, by the president or pastor, of information from within the organization. And in a financial crisis maybe, just maybe, corporate prayer could be given first priority over cost-cutting.

This is a major step for a Christian organization to take, one in which it identifies with its own people and undertakes to eliminate the oppressive conditions that cause them such grief. It is an essential step for every Christian organization to take. But there is also another. The Christian organization must step outside its own boundaries and reach out to the poor. The biblical mandate is that we make some provision for the poor.

To give an example, the Scott Bader Company has successfully managed to bring justice to oppressive conditions both inside and outside the company.[27] It was established in 1920, and it was the desire of the founder to create a Christian way of life in his business. The Scott Bader Company was also established on the idea of common wealth, which was formalized by instituting the Scott Bader Commonwealth.

Over the course of the next forty years, the company became a leading producer of polyester resins and other chemical products and went through two revolutionary changes: a complete transformation of ownership and a voluntary acceptance of self-denying ordinances. To implement the first, the Scott Bader Company went from mere profit sharing to common ownership with the employees, thus the name Commonwealth. To achieve the second, a constitution was written to restrict the firm's freedom of action. One provision of particular note was that remuneration for work within the organization could not vary by more than a 1:7 ratio of the lowest paid to the highest paid. This has solid biblical backup in the manna story in Exodus 16, referred to by Paul: " He that gathered much did not have too much, and he that gathered little did not have too little."[28]

A second noteworthy provision was that the board of directors of the operating company, the Scott Bader Company, was made fully accountable to the common ownership, the Scott Bader Commonwealth. A third noteworthy provision was the truly remarkable requirement that twenty percent of company profits were to be given to charitable purposes outside the organization. The main focus of that giving through the years has been to help those that society neglects—the forgotten people. The company has heeded Ezekiel's great warning, to grasp the hand of the poor and needy.[29] They have not gathered all the wealth for themselves.

As other examples, there also are churches that have gotten outside their own boundaries and grasped the hand of the poor:

In New York City, the former Episcopal Bishop, Horace W. B. Donegan, announced that there would be no further work on the Cathedral of St. John the Divine "until there is greater evidence that the anguish and despair of our unadvantaged people has been relieved."

In the state of Washington, the pastor of a small-town Lutheran church called the headquarters of the Lutheran Relief Service in New York to say that his congregation would soon be sending them a check for $100,000. "We decided to borrow the money," he told the astonished chief administrator. "We figured that we'd be willing to do it for a church addition, so why not for the world's starving people?"[30]

Blessing Others

In the end, the ingredient that we add to the kettle that gives it the flavor of servanthood more than any of the other ingredients is *sacrifice*. The extent to which we can sacrifice for others is the extent to which we will be their servant.

Putting others first is not natural. We usually turn it around, by serving ourselves first and seeing to it that we get what we want. Then we tack on service to others, either out of our sense of Christian duty or to round out our résumé. We rationalize: How can I possibly help others if I am not first on top of things myself?

We may feel that we must accomplish great things so we can establish ourselves as being *successful*—then people will know we have something to offer and can be of help. Or we may strive to be accepted by others, hoping to be *popular*—then we can stretch ourselves on behalf of others without fear of rejection. Or, maybe we choose to become *powerful*—anticipating that once we acquire enough power, we can manipulate conditions to help people without having to get involved with them.

Whatever our reason for putting ourselves first so we can create the best possible situation for helping others, it will never match the instructions found in Scripture: "Each of you should look not only to your own interests, but also to the interests of others."[31] Period. Our interests and the interests of others go together, both individually and corporately. For example, serving one another within our group and serving others outside of our group are not contingent upon what we can accomplish, how well we are accepted, or how much power we can acquire. Instead, serving one another and serving others are contingent upon self-sacrifice in the three areas just mentioned, so that we can be a blessing to others.

Henri Nouwen uses Christ's temptations in the desert to infuse the concept of servanthood with these three areas of self-sacrifice.[32] The first temptation, to turn stones into bread, was really a temptation to be successful, or relevant. Just as Christ did not yield to the temptation to be relevant, Nouwen arrives at the conclusion that the servant leader or worker must not either—the rather startling conclusion that the servant leader or worker must be irrelevant. What one has to offer is not one's accomplishments but only one's own vulnerable self.

Christian leaders and workers want to fight the simplicity of that. Are we not called to change lives through the power of the Holy Spirit and to show the world that our ministry makes a difference to God's glory? Aren't we trying to have an impact so we know that what we are doing is significant and worthwhile? How easily it shifts, though, into the piling up of results to prove that we're doing a good job. And to whose power and glory is it now? No, we are not called to prove our prowess but to proclaim God's love—just as Jesus did.

Jesus' second and third temptations had to do with popularity and power. And again, in following Jesus we do not need to elevate ourselves to the status of organizational hero by doing something especially significant and worthwhile so that we can be popular. In truth, I think of the organizational hero as one who has grandiose dreams and spectacular schemes that drain the organization's resources and demand that others pick up the pieces, and one who makes exciting promises to all who are inspired by his or her vision for the future. I see a rather pathetic person in all of that, overreaching his or her own abilities and the abilities of others, trying desperately to be loved and to return love in some measure but opting for power over love and ending up with an empire instead.

Why do power and love conflict like that? Maybe Nouwen has it right:

> Power offers an easy substitute for the hard task of love . . . . The long painful history of the Church is the history of people ever and again tempted to choose power over love, control over the cross, being a leader over being led. Those who resisted this temptation to the end and thereby give us hope are the true saints.
>
> One thing is clear to me: the temptation of power is greatest when intimacy is a threat. Much Christian leadership is exercised by people who do not know how to develop healthy, intimate relationships and have opted for power and control instead.

Many Christian empire-builders have been people unable to give and receive love.[33]

Am I willing to give up my desire to be relevant, my desire to be popular, and my desire for power? Now we are touching the most important quality of servanthood: being ready to follow Jesus wherever He guides you. Jesus said, "I tell you most solemnly, when you were young you put on your belt and walked where you liked; but when you grow old you will stretch out your hands and somebody else will put a belt around you and take you where you would rather not go."[34]

The world has it the other way around. When you were young, you always had to do what other people wanted, ask permission to do what you wanted, and jump through all kinds of hoops to get to where you are today. But now you supposedly can do what you want. You have "earned the right" to control your own destiny.

Jesus, however, has a different proposition for you, and it is the ultimate sacrifice. It is this: Be willing to give up control of your destiny. Be willing to be led where you would rather not go.

This, of course, does not mean that you should agree to being victimized by a neurotic boss, an addictive organization or a spiritually abusive pastor. The Holy Spirit will give you your own discernment and counsel from others to keep you from being led where you *should not* go. On the other hand, the Holy Spirit will also give you an awareness of the needs of others. That is how He will show you where you *should* go. Then, as you serve others, the responses you get will help determine how to proceed further.

Don't be surprised if you end up being served by the one you are serving.[35] Let's use as an example the mutuality of leading and following. This is a process that begins with the leader's awareness of and sensitivity to the needs of those that he or she is serving. This not only mobilizes the followers' needs but also arouses hopes and aspirations that those needs will be met. Next comes a period of engagement between the leader's and followers' motivations: a period that transforms both. In fact, the transformation ends up being complete enough in some cases that the followers turn around and serve the leader in some areas in which the leader has now developed needs. Technically, this is called "transformational leadership," and it is a nice description of the transformational nature and mutuality of serving others.

Being willing to be led by those we serve to where we would rather not go—that is the sacrificial spirit of servanthood that could transform an entire organization practically overnight. As Christian leaders and workers, we are not called to go only where we want to go. We are called to be servants, working in concert with all of God's people, with each person as he or she is gifted, to bring glory to God and to further His kingdom.

King Rehoboam in the Old Testament did not do it that way, and we need to learn from his experience. In 1 Kings 12, we read that the whole assembly of Israel came to him and asked him to lighten their load, the unbearable yoke laid upon them by his father, King Solomon. The elders' advice to Rehoboam, when he asked for it, agreed with the people's suggestion.

But Rehoboam did what many leaders do today. He gathered and "conferred with the young men who grew up with him and who stood by him" (v. 8)—his cronies, who would tell him what he wanted to hear. And they did. They advised Rehoboam to tell the people, "My little finger is thicker than my father's loins" (v. 10). In other words, let them know you're tough. You're the boss. So Rehoboam, doing what was right in his own eyes rather than what was truly right, "spoke harshly to the people, disregarding the advice given him by the elders" (v. 13).

The story continues: "When all Israel saw that the king paid no attention to them, the people sent back this message to the king: 'What share have we in David? We have no heritage in Jesse's son. To your tents, O Israel! Look now after your own house, O David!' " (v. 16). And verse 15 tells us that this tragic turn of events was from the Lord. Just what was the elders' advice? "If you will be a servant to this people now and serve them and reply to them with kind words, they will always be your servants" (v. 7).[36] That is transformational leadership, and it is servant leadership. Too bad Rehoboam didn't "get it"!

The calling is the same for leader and follower alike: to empty oneself in the service of others—to follow Jesus. Whether the organization you are in is neurotic, addictive or spiritually abusive, or even if it is an empowering organization, your calling as a Christian is to empty yourself and to be a blessing to others.

Be willing to empty yourself. This sacrifice finds its finest expression in the biblical concept of hospitality.[37] Biblical hospitality can occur in any organization—whether in the workplace or place of worship—when emptying yourself creates an atmosphere that allows others to work or worship without fear or hostility. Anyone, at any level of the organization, can create this kind of an atmosphere. However, you must begin with those people with whom you are in competition and from whom you are estranged. It is with these people that you must empty yourself of your own hostilities and fears, setting your rivalries and suspicions aside—sacrificing your self-protective defenses, whatever the risk may be.

Employers, employees, pastors, parishioners—all must empty themselves to be good hosts. According to Nouwen, the process involves *poverty* and *receptivity*. It means inviting others into your world without imposing your viewpoint on them. It means not "anxiously clinging to our private property, whatever it is: our knowledge, our good name, our land, our money, or the many objects we have collected around us."[38] Or, I would add, our title, our position, our expertise or our spiritual maturity. In Nouwen's words, "poverty makes a good host."[39]

The good host is not filled with his or her own perceptions, expectations and theologies. Nor is the good host preoccupied with complaining when such things are threatened. Rather, hospitality involves developing enough inner space to make room for the other person's perceptions, expectations, theologies—and complaints. In short, discovering what he or she is about.

But the good host is not just a "neutral nobody"; or, in other words, "an empty house is not a hospitable house":

> To be receptive to the stranger in no way implies that we have to become neutral "nobodies." Real receptivity asks for

confrontation because space can only be a welcoming space when there are clear boundaries, and boundaries are limits between which we define our own position. Flexible limits, but limits nonetheless. Confrontation results from the articulate presence, the presence within boundaries, of the host to the guest by which he offers himself as a point of orientation and a frame of reference. We are not hospitable when we leave our house to strangers and let them use it any way they want. An empty house is not a hospitable house.[40]

Similarly, an open mind is not an empty mind. To not define one's position, to not be an articulate presence, and to fail to offer oneself as a point of orientation and frame of reference is to fail to truly be a blessing to others.

To be a genuinely good host, you must not only empty yourself but also expose yourself. You must not only create a free and friendly atmosphere uncompromised by fear and hostility, but you must also be an active witness to the knowledge and insight, good sense, and judgment learned from your faithful walk with the Lord. You must always be prepared to bring Christ into the relationship as a living testimony, as living evidence that Christ is alive and that following Him really does make a difference. You must remain true to Scripture: "That . . . which we have heard, which we have seen with our eyes, which we have looked at and our hands have touched—this we proclaim."[41]

You must, as a wounded Christian worker, hold onto your Christian commitment and convictions in the midst of your torment. You must hold fast to your calling to follow Jesus and hold yourself and your leaders accountable to standards that honor God as you lovingly serve those around you.

Take a little time right now to think these things through. Up to this point, you have analyzed the negative aspects of your organization and have had an opportunity to review the concept of empowerment and the five ideal servant-qualities of Christian leadership. In other words, you now know how things are and how they should be. You will need to have the latter very clearly in mind if you plan to do anything about the former.

In the heat of the battle, is it hard sometimes to remember your Christian perspective? Is it difficult to make sense out of who you are, working or worshiping in the place where you are? Are you beginning to lose some of your Christian convictions and to lose sight of what biblically compatible non-Christian organizations and Christ-centered Christian organizations should be like?

You need to have firmly imprinted on your heart your commitment to who you are as a Christian and your convictions of what an organization should be, especially one that claims to be Christian. When the two come together—when you have a vision in your heart that Christian is Christian regardless of its individual or corporate form—then you will be ready to proclaim God's word in the midst of Babylon.

Write out, in two or three paragraphs, your ideal organization. Is it consistent with who you are as a Christian? We will come back to it later when we go to work figuring out what action you should take to complete your recovery process.

PHASE
THREE

RESPONDING

8

Ministering
to Others

WHEN YOU TREAT PEOPLE AS THEY ARE, you make them worse than
they are. When you treat them as if they already were what
they potentially could be, you make them what they should be.
Goethe said something like that many years ago. It applies just as
well to us today as we struggle with the tension between what is
and what should be.

You now know more clearly than before what it is really like
for you where you work or worship. You know what kind of an
organization you are dealing with and what you bring to it that
perhaps makes matters worse. You also have a better idea of how
things should be—what the organization ideally would be like if it
were at least biblically compatible, if not totally and thoroughly
Christian through and through.

You are also a wounded worker. And you know that you must
take action to work your way out of the self-perpetuating cycle of
fear that keeps you stuck in your woundedness. First, you want
release from the madness or badness that surrounds you, but fear
takes over. What if you quit and can't find a new job? What if you
change churches and the same old thing happens all over again?

So you turn to thoughts of relief—how you can change things to make them better right where you are. And fear stops you again. Maybe if you were to just leave . . . and around and around it goes.

What can you do? First, stop treating your employer or pastor as he or she is, or your job or church as it is. Resolve to start treating them as if they already are what they potentially could be: biblically compatible or totally and thoroughly Christian in all that they do.

Second, remember who you are in the Lord, and do not compromise what He has shown you. You have put your job or church to the test, and you have put yourself to the test. You recognize your situation for what it is. You have reaffirmed or reclaimed your Christian identity and your Christian ideals. By doing so, you have drunk the Cup of Blessing. Now you must refuse to compromise your trust in the Lord. In other words, drink the Cup of Acceptance, and give witness to what you know to be true.

Probably nothing could be harder than what I have just said. Fear of making matters worse, fear of repercussions and the hopelessness that nothing you do will make any difference anyway take the wind out of your sails pretty fast. That is because you may think of witnessing as correcting others, telling them what they should believe or how they should act. In this case, that is not what I mean.

If you tell others their faults, pointing out their weaknesses and where they are wrong, you are treating them as they are, and you will quite possibly make them worse. If you show them a better way, within the context of following Christ, you will be treating them as if they already were totally committed to following Christ in everything that they do, and they will quite possibly get better. (That is, hopefully they will get better, at least to some degree, but there are no guarantees.) This is where the ministry of abiding comes in. We will consider it in two of its forms: abiding as a *prophetic witness* and abiding as a *wounded healer.*

Abiding as a Prophetic Witness

Let's start with what you already know and build a foundation for the ministry of abiding as a prophetic witness. You know what is and what should be. You know your calling as a Christian and what an ideal organization is: If it is non-Christian, it is at least biblically compatible; and if it is Christian, it is more than just Christian in name only. Your witness is to what God has shown you for the situation that He has given you. He has given you the situation, you have not. Unfortunately, I have seen more poor "witness to the truth" in this one area than in any other. Some overzealous Christians assume they are God's gift to the situation and nothing will change without their input. And nothing can stop them. They are full of accusations and exhortations. They are speaking for God and will not be stilled.

Does that sound like a prophetic witness? It certainly could be. It can be abused, but God does at times give organizations certain gifted persons to accuse and exhort without ceasing. And nothing will change unless the people listen. We see many examples in Scripture of that very thing.

However, I want you to be aware that there is another form of prophetic witnessing. It is showing, not telling. It is weeping for, not wailing at. Scripture upholds this view as well. Jeremiah, the "weeping prophet," wrote two books of the Old Testament. One is titled the Book of Lamentations. Jesus, too, wept.

In chapter 7, I stated that the witness of grieving is the strongest statement that can be made of things not being right. As a wounded Christian worker, when you reveal your pain, it is testimony to the fact that what you see is not pleasing to God. You are weeping because you belong to Christ, and in living for Christ He is living through you. Christ is weeping through you.

The announcement that one of Christ's own has been hurt personally, or is hurting on behalf of others, should send shock waves through the organization. What could possibly be more important than tending the sheep? Many don't see it that way. "We must go on and put this behind us." "The ministry of the whole is too important to let this divert our attention." "It is important for this ministry to survive, and there will be casualties along the way. We can't help that." I strongly disagree.

What others say is not your responsibility. Your responsibility is to be faithful, as a follower of Christ, to give prophetic witness to what you know to be true. It may fall on deaf ears, but be faithful to your calling. Notice that as you are faithful in your witness, change takes place in you. Now there is meaning to your woundedness. Finally, your wounds are meaningful to you because they represent the opportunity God has given to you to further His kingdom. You have taken up your cross, and your life is filled with meaning.

In addition, you may begin to be heard and to be given opportunities to express your expectations as a follower of Christ. If so, speak simply as one who loves the Lord to another who loves the Lord. Share what would be uplifting to you as a Christian and empowering to you as a Christian worker in that organization or in a given situation.

You might say something like the following:

- "I appreciate it when we have a healthy give and take on issues, rather than feeling that to disagree is to be disrespectful."
- "I would appreciate it if we would pray together before decisions are made that affect us."
- "I prefer not to compete with someone to get ahead at his or her expense. Instead, I will be supportive and share whatever I can so we can both be successful."
- "It is upsetting to me when one position on a multifaceted matter is presented as biblically mandated, when actually there are other positions that Christians could take."
- "I would hope we would never fall back on un-Christlike means to achieving our ends, like dishonesty or unfairness, caricaturing of those who disagree, misrepresenting opposing views, or prejudging people without hearing their side."

You will be able to think of other things to say as the occasion arises. You are simply sharing your commitment and perspective as an act of personal accountability to be Christlike in everything you do, hoping that your workplace or place of worship will not discourage you and diminish your walk with the Lord. Your boss or pastor may or may not respond appropriately. That is not your responsibility.

Your responsibility, again, is to be faithful to your calling. You know the way things should be, biblically, in an organization, and you know you are acting accordingly. You are providing a prophetic witness as an encouragement to your boss or pastor to also follow Christ, or biblically compatible values and beliefs, in everything that he or she does. You are not providing a prophetic witness as a condemnation of everything that he or she does wrong. You are crying out as one of the oppressed and singing a new song of hope. You are engaging in the intentional ministry of singing "the Lord's song in a strange land"[1] without compromising your trust in the Lord. You are abiding as a prophetic witness.

Your response is not one of either fight or flight, but of carrying the freight. Abiding is not working to change one's own situation or relieving someone else of his or her burden directly. Nor is it moving away from the conflict. Rather, abiding is first of all taking on the weight of the situation and of other people's burdens as a focus for concern, not change. With the focus off change, per se, the agenda then becomes faithful witnessing to what God is calling you to and to what a quality organization is really like.

Change can result from the ministry of abiding, but it is because of broader changes in a leader's attitude or behavior, or in an organization's culture. For example, as you are steadfast and persevere in your witness to how you should be treated as a Christian in a Christian organization and how the organization should conduct itself so as not to be Christian in name only, the leadership may be encouraged to wake up to the call to follow Christ in all that they do. Or they may not. But you just keep on. That is what abiding is all about.

Some have the idea that abiding is putting your tail between your legs, keeping a stiff upper lip, burying your head in the sand, not rocking the boat, and just waiting it out. Just see it through— this, too, shall pass. They are wrong. Abiding is not passive. It is active. It is staying in your situation, whatever it is, and actively dwelling there, making it as hospitable as you can. It is an act of servanthood, of bearing with others' faults rather than bearing down on them. It is an act of prophetic witness, of enduring others' pain, and of encouraging Christian oppressors to follow Christ or non-Christian oppressors to follow biblically compatible values and beliefs in all that they do.

ABIDING AS A WOUNDED HEALER

Abiding is actively waiting for tomorrow. It is not an idle pastime. Nor is it done in isolation. In order to endure the pain of others, you must enter into the pain of a specific other person. You will not truly understand the collective pain by compiling rumors and assembling the big picture from lots of little story fragments from over here and over there. Nor will you qualify to speak for the needs of the many in this way. You become a prophetic witness by personally entering into communion with the human suffering of a specific individual or individuals.

At this point, you also become a wounded healer.[2] By entering into others' suffering with them, you are creating a context for healing. Your own suffering has brought you to the place of their suffering, where you can dwell together. You are waiting for them there, where they have been so alone. They have had no one waiting for them before, either for today or for tomorrow. Now they have you. You have become their tomorrow.

Waiting for tomorrow together is healing to you as well. Abiding is a healing ministry that works both ways. It works for you because it draws you out of yourself. Now your restless grief has been exposed to the light of day, so you can no longer deny its existence. Nor can you wallow in it. Your numbness has turned to witness, and your life once again is filled with meaning. Your wounds have become God-given opportunities for prophetic witness to your leaders, as I mentioned earlier, or in this case to your peers. You are showing them a better way—abiding—and weeping with them as you wait for tomorrow together. You are a wounded healer.

What, more precisely, does it take to be a wounded healer? I will list three things: clarification, compassion and contemplation.

Clarification

The first task is to be able to clarify the confusion of people who are consumed with pain and need to understand why things are the way they are. Many people in pain are residing in an inner world of thought and emotion with which they are not familiar. They are not prepared to encounter all they find there and to also find strength there to move ahead with their lives.

The wounded healer must be prepared. You must have already lessened your own confusion by giving names to your painful experiences and recognizing your own victimization. These need to no longer be obstacles to moving ahead with your own life but must become opportunities to help others move ahead with theirs. Only if you are able to clarify your own experience, will you be able to offer yourself as a source of clarification to others.

There is one area in particular that I would suggest you check. It is what has been referred to as the Inner Saul. Let me share a story with you. It is about a mad king, Saul by name, and a young shepherd named David:

> The mad king saw David as a threat to the *king's* kingdom. The king did not understand, it seems, that God should be left to decide what kingdoms survive which threats. Not knowing this, Saul did what all mad kings do. He threw spears at David. He could. *He* was king. Kings can do things like that. They almost always do. Kings claim the right to throw spears. . . .
>
> Is it possible that this mad king was the *true* king, even the Lord's anointed?
>
> What about your king? Is he the Lord's anointed? Maybe he is. Maybe he isn't. No one can ever really know for sure. Men

say they are sure. Even *certain*. But they are not. They do *not* know. God knows. But *He* will not tell.

If your king is truly the Lord's anointed, and if he *also* throws spears, then there are some things you *can* know, and know for sure:

Your king is quite mad.

And he is a king after the order of King Saul. . . .

As the king grew in madness, David grew in understanding. He knew that God had placed him in the king's palace, under true authority.

The authority of King Saul, *true*? Yes, God's chosen authority. *Chosen for David.* Unbroken authority, yes. But divine in ordination, nonetheless.

Yes, *that* is possible.

David drew in his breath, placed himself under his mad king, and moved farther down the path of his earthly hell.

David had a question: What do you do when someone throws a spear at you?. . .

What can a man, especially a young man, do when the king decides to use him for target practice? What if the young man decides not to return the compliment?

First of all, he must pretend he cannot see spears. Even when they are coming straight at him. Secondly, he must also learn to duck very quickly. Lastly, he must pretend nothing at all happened.

You can easily tell when someone has been hit by a spear. He turns a deep shade of bitter. David never got hit. Gradually, he learned a very well kept secret. He discovered three things that prevented him from ever being hit.

One, never learn anything about the fashionable, easily-mastered art of spear throwing. Two, stay out of the company of all spear throwers. And three, keep your mouth tightly closed.

In this way, spears will never touch you, even when they pierce your heart. . . .

"I'm in David's situation, and I am in agony. What do I do when the kingdom I'm in is ruled by a spear-wielding king?" . . .

You have your eyes on the wrong King Saul. As long as you look at your king, you will blame him, and him alone, for your

present hell. Be careful, for God has *His* eyes fastened sharply
on another King Saul. Not the visible one standing up there
throwing spears at you. No, God is looking at *another* King
Saul. One just as bad—or worse.

King Saul is looking at the King Saul in *you.* . . .

King Saul is one with you.

You are King Saul!

He breathes in the lungs and beats in the breast of all of us.
There is only one way to get rid of him. He must be annihilated.

You may not particularly find this to be a compliment, but
at least now you know why God put you under someone who
just *might* be King Saul.

David the sheepherder would have grown up to become King
Saul II, except that God cut away the Saul inside David's heart.
The operation, by the way, took years and was a brutalizing
experience that almost killed the patient. And what were the
scalpel and tongs God used to remove this inner Saul?

God used the outer Saul.

King Saul sought to destroy David, but his only success was
that he became the handmaiden of God to put to death the Saul
who roamed about in the caverns of David's own soul.[3]

Have you clarified your Inner Saul? Do you know what to do
when your king throws spears at you? Do you turn "a deep shade
of bitter?" Do you return thrown spears? Do you "have your eyes
on the wrong King Saul?"

Is your boss or your pastor the Lord's anointed, and is he or
she after the order of Saul? Is he or she God's chosen instrument
to cut away the King Saul inside your heart? As long as you blame
your boss or your pastor, and him or her alone, for your present
hell, you will miss the other King Saul: the one in you. God's
purpose is to use the Outer Saul—the one throwing the spears—
to remove the Inner Saul—the one who would throw them back.
Wounded healers are not wounded spear-throwers.

Compassion

The second task of the wounded healer is to recognize that the
craving for justice that your neighbor feels also resides in your

own heart, and that the cruel desire to get even is also rooted in your own impulses. It is through compassion that you sense the Inner Saul in your neighbor's eyes, which are focused on the wrong King Saul. You, too, have wept in your agony, while through your tears you dodge spears and fight the temptation to throw one back.

Compassion prepares the way for forgiveness. Compassion demonstrates to your neighbor that the sins of the enemy are in the hearts of everyone, and that the answer does not lie in the spear but in the cross. Your testimony is to the two-step process that stopped your bleeding and prepared the way for your own healing. First, Jesus forgave you. Second, you forgave others. The second step was yours to take. You were not free from the restrictive chains of shame and anxiety, nor were you free to fully accept God's promise that you have a future and a hope, until you took up your cross and forgave your enemy. Healing starts when the bleeding stops.

Compassion points to the possibility of forgiving the leader who does not measure up to what a leader should be, but who is doing the best that he or she can. Compassion says to let go, as I have. Take your eyes off the Outer Saul. Turn your eyes upon Jesus. Forgive, and begin your recovery.

I must caution you. Do not confuse compassion with something else. Beware of a form of spiritual exhibitionism that is extremely popular today. It is most pronounced among Christian speakers, authors, preachers and entertainers, who vividly portray their own woundedness as the fuel that drives their message. It makes it easier to identify with them and adds to their credibility. And it stirs the passions. But it is not a message of compassion. Listen to the wise counsel of Henri Nouwen:

> A minister who talks in the pulpit about his own personal problems is of no help to his congregation, for no suffering human being is helped by someone who tells him that he has the same problems. Remarks such as, "Don't worry because I suffer from the same depression, confusion and anxiety as you

do," help no one. This spiritual exhibitionism adds little faith to little faith and creates narrow-mindedness instead of new perspectives. Open wounds stink and do not heal.[4]

Wounded workers do not become wounded healers by keeping others' wounds open so they cannot heal. The agenda of the wounded healer is to stop the bleeding so that healing may begin.

Contemplation

The third task of the wounded healer is to discern dysfunctional individual and organizational realities and look for signs of hope. You must be careful, however, not to become absorbed in the personal and corporate tragedies that you discover. You must not, in Nouwen's words "shoulder every protest sign" to show that you truly care or submit to every reactionary impulse to prove that you understand. You must "keep a certain distance," so that your witness is not contaminated by the "panic-stricken convulsions" of those without hope.

The wounded healer needs to maintain a contemplative space, yet a compassionate space. This is not an empty space but an articulate presence, the mark of hospitality whereby the host offers himself / herself to the guest as a point of orientation and frame of reference (as discussed in chapter 7). I want to emphasize the fact, however, that there is a limit, as expressed by the following:

> Why is this a healing ministry? It is healing because it takes away the false illusion that wholeness can be given by one to another. It is healing because it does not take away . . . the pain of another, but invites him to recognize his [pain] on a level where it can be shared. Many people in this life suffer because they are anxiously searching for the man or woman, the event or encounter, which will take their [pain] away. But when they enter a house with real hospitality they soon see that their own wounds must be understood not as sources of despair and bitterness, but as signs that they have to travel on in obedience to the calling sounds of their own wounds.[5]

As a wounded healer, you are not called to ride in on a white horse, take away the pain, and ride off into the sunset. Instead, you are called to come alongside, and (a) clarify the confusion of thoughts and feelings, (b) prepare the way for forgiveness, and (c) discern dysfunctional realities and look for signs of hope. Wait for tomorrow together with those God has called you to minister to, and let "the calling sounds of their own wounds" be their guide, as you share together the journey from heartache to recovery.

IS ABIDING FOR YOU?

Look back at your test results in chapters 3–5. If your responses to the Organization Tests were primarily in the *Never* category, and your responses to the Self Tests indicated that your personality is basically compatible with your situation, abiding may be your best strategy. Also review the information on the dysfunctional personality, the codependent personality and the demonically influenced personality. Consider your responses to the questions that were asked. You may want to consult the suggested readings or perhaps see a counselor. This can help regardless of the strategy you choose.

Think about what abiding as a prophetic witness or a wounded healer entails. Consider the following questions:

1. Are you comfortable expressing your expectations as a follower of Christ?
2. Are you careful not to judge your boss or pastor whenever he or she does something wrong?
3. Are you able to endure the pain of others and encourage their oppressors to follow Christ in all that they do?
4. Have you clarified your Inner Saul?
5. Are you able to resist spiritual exhibitionism?
6. Are you able to withstand becoming so absorbed in other people's problems that you cannot discern dysfunctional reality and look for signs of hope?

Your answers to these questions will help you make abiding work for you. There is, now, one more question you must answer. It is based on the assumption that wounded healers recognize the sufferings of their own heart as the starting point for their ministry to other wounded workers. The question is this: How do you view suffering?

Philip Yancey has discovered at least five biblical approaches to suffering.[6] He views them as a progression of stages. Which stage represents your view of suffering?

1. **A person who lives right should not have to suffer.** This is the easiest one to come up with. It's almost automatic for the wounded worker to say, "I've been doing my job faithfully. I never had an idea anything was wrong. How can they do this to me?" Yancey says:

> We should at least acknowledge that similar sentiments do appear in the Bible, especially in the Book of Proverbs, which implies that right living will earn its reward *in this life*. And consider the sweeping promise of Psalm 1:3 to the righteous man: "Whatever he does prospers."

Yancey notes that God guaranteed prosperity in his covenant with Israel, if they would faithfully follow Him. He adds:

> But the Israelites broke the terms of the covenant, and a book like the Psalms reveals the Jews' anguished adjustment to new realities. Almost a third of the psalms show a "righteous" author struggling with the failure of prosperity theology.

2. **Good people suffer, but they will find relief.** The wounded worker at this stage will say, "If I just hang in there and keep on doing what's right, things will get better." Scripture does tell of many faithful persons who were relieved of their suffering at one time or another. But it didn't always work out that way. There was One in particular who did not find relief on this earth: Jesus. He died.

3. All things work together for good. This is usually good but incomplete advice. It doesn't go far enough. The good that is to come may not be for today or even tomorrow. With reference to Romans 8, Yancey puts this stage, and the first two stages, into perspective:

> Paul found a neat way to resolve the contradictions raised by the first two . . . stages. Hardship is part of the human condition, and no one can claim an exemption. But for those who love God, the condition is temporary. One day the "groaning" creation will be liberated, and all hardship will be abolished. We have a timing problem, Paul says. Just wait: God's miracle of transforming Bad Friday into Easter Sunday will be enlarged to cosmic scale.

4. Faithful people may be called to suffer. Sometimes this kind of advice is given to a wounded person: "If your faith were not so strong, you would not be tested like this." This assumes that if we faithfully follow Christ, we will suffer unjustly. According to Scripture, particularly 1 Peter, that's right.

5. To live is Christ and to die is gain. How many wounded workers can honestly say that? Paul was a wounded Christian worker, and he said it in his letter to the Philippians. His was the ultimate view of suffering: Regardless of the circumstances, the single all-surpassing goal is to exalt Christ. To live is Christ, to die is gain.

Which stage represents your view of suffering? Are you stuck at Stage One, telling yourself over and over that you didn't deserve it? Are you at Stage Two, telling yourself that if you just hang in there, sooner or later the suffering has to stop? The wounded healer must rise above both of these views, which strongly suggest that suffering and righteousness do not go together. True ministry to others is not possible unless suffering is seen as integral to the human condition.

Are you at Stage Three? Do you accept suffering as part of the human condition and believe that relief in the temporal sense is secondary to relief in the eternal sense? Do you show others that you are willing to wait for tomorrow together? Be careful, I might add, to not take acceptance of suffering too far: "In its worst form this teaching denies the vileness of evil and baptizes the most horrible tragedies as the will of God. Scripture commands us to live in a spirit of thanksgiving in the midst of all situations; it does not command us to celebrate the presence of evil."[7]

Are you at Stage Four? Do you believe that relief is not the issue, but endurance is? Do you tell others that the stronger their faith is the more it will be put to the test, and, additionally, that they will not be tested beyond their Christ-empowered ability to endure?

Or, are you at Stage Five? If you are, you have been unusually empowered by God. The ultimate view for the Christian is that all of life, whatever it brings, is Christ, and even when it leads to death, it merely brings more of Him.

Consider very carefully where you stand regarding the issue of suffering. It will greatly affect your ability to minister as a wounded healer. If you have not moved past Stage Two, you probably have not moved past the quick fix of instant relief, which is telling a fellow wounded worker that although he has lost his job, he has great kids and his wife loves him. That's pretty shallow considering the depth of his pain!

Abiding is not easy. I say that with respect for the depth of your own pain as a wounded worker/healer. But the only way to recover from your woundedness is by constructively responding to it. I have listed some possibilities for you in this chapter. Some are directed outward to help others heal and become more Christlike. Some are directed inward to help you heal yourself.

Abiding is a choice among alternatives. It is not what is left by default. To do nothing is not to abide. Abiding is an active response that furthers God's kingdom. Perhaps, however, you do not feel ready, and you would prefer to put your recovery on hold while you work on your own position in His kingdom. Hopefully, you have gained enough insight to know what issues you need to work on.

Or, it may be that the problems in your organization are too troubling to let them continue without a more decisive response.

You may have concluded that you don't feel led to minister to others right now, but you would rather make some changes or perhaps even move on to something else. Maybe you would like to be a *change* agent and get the show on the road. Or perhaps you would prefer to become a *free* agent and hit the road, leaving your troubles behind. We'll consider these two alternatives next.

Making Changes

IT USUALLY COMES DOWN TO THIS: fight or flight. Do I fight the battle, or do I flee the battlefield? Do I stand up for what is right or stomp out with righteous indignation? Should I try to make changes or just move on?

Few decisions are harder to make than this one. One possible scenario is that you've been with your company for years, and now you can see that it is clearly a neurotic organization. You can't take the favoritism and fear, or your feelings of shame, rage and estrangement any longer.

Another possible scenario is that you're committed to a school's mission, and you love teaching, but you're beginning to realize that the school's lofty ideals are being used to hide the fact that basic biblical principles are not being applied in actual practice. You've also come to the realization that although you love teaching, there is only one reason you continue to teach at a Christian school. You are not being paid a competitive wage, but you know your reward will be in heaven. You have become motivated solely by the power of the promise, which means you're working in an addictive organization. You're wondering how you can break the spell.

A third possibility is that you've been an active member of your church for several years. You've grown as a Christian and contributed many hours of dedicated service to ministry. But now you're beginning to notice things that don't seem right: power-posturing, preoccupation with performance, lack of balance, misplaced loyalty, paranoia and secretiveness. Your church is spiritually abusive. What should you do?

ARE YOU A CHANGE AGENT?

First, turn back to chapters 3–5. Review your responses to the tests for neurotic, addictive and spiritually abusive organizations. Look particularly at the items marked *Sometimes*. These are problems that are bothersome enough to warrant change but not so intolerable as to be overwhelming. The exact number of them that you marked is not important. Circle the ones you would like to see changed.

Second, look over your responses to the Self Tests in chapters 3–5. Note the items marked *Yes*. Again, the exact number is not the point. Would they interfere with or neutralize your ability to work for change? Cross out the items marked *Sometimes* that you circled for change that are incompatible with your personality.

Third, look back over chapters 6 and 7 for aspects of the ideal organization that you would like to see in your organization. Read your two- or three-paragraph description at the end of chapter 7. What items for change would you add to your list that includes the remaining circled items in chapters 3–5? Let's call that your *Change List*.

Now pause for a moment and ask yourself the following questions:[1]

1. Does grace have a chance? Or are things just too far gone? Is there a possibility that things could change?
2. Are you supporting what you hate? If you believe it is wrong, why do you support it?
3. Do you need to be right? Are you locked in a no-win war of wills to prove who is right? Are you consumed with proving your point, and is that why you are sticking it out?

4. Can you stay, and stay healthy? If you stay, can your wounds heal?

5. Can you set your own limits? Can you decide on how much time and effort you are willing to invest in being an agent of change, and can you stick with it?

6. Do you feel it is up to you to fix all the problems? Or do you believe that God can expose lies and resolve injustices without you?

7. Is it possible that the organization should die? Has the glory of the Lord departed? If so, what effect would your staying or leaving have?

8. Are you going to try to help even though you are emotionally exhausted? Can you help others find peace when you can't find peace yourself?

9. Are you able to listen to other perspectives? Talk with people who have already left because they saw what you see. What are their perspectives now?

10. Do you know where to sow? Is your organization hard soil, rocky soil, thorny soil or good soil? Is the problem the fact that you have not spoken the truth well enough or long enough, or is it that the soil is bad?

11. If you came today to your organization for the first time, knowing what you now know about it, would you stay?

12. If you stay, can you remember whom you really serve? Are you clear about your identity in Christ and your calling to follow Him in everything that you do?

13. If you try to change the system, are you ready for resistance? Can you keep focused on Christ while you are being personally attacked?

14. Can you keep telling the truth? Can you cast your burdens upon Christ and receive the power from Him to endure?

15. Do you know who the enemy is? Are you aware that spiritual warfare may be involved, in addition to the obvious human problems that you see in the leadership and life of the organization?

These are pretty sobering thoughts for you to consider as you decide whether to keep on or move on. If, after reflecting on them, you believe the Lord is telling you to stay, then join me as I take a closer look at that last question—about spiritual warfare.

Do You Know Who the Enemy Is?

You have essentially three choices. You can focus your energies for change on the leadership. Or you can focus on the organization itself. Or you can focus on the spiritual realm that encompasses the entire organization and everything about it and everyone within it. It is a very important choice for you to make, because if you make the wrong choice, you could win the battle and lose the war.

The tendency most often is to zero in on the manager, chairperson, boss or pastor who hurt you. Most people think, "If I could just get him or her to change, everything would be okay again." As I pointed out in the previous chapter, however, if you treat people as though they are what they should be, rather than what they actually are, perhaps you can make them better. If you merely try to change their faults, perhaps you'll make them worse.

A direct frontal attack is usually viewed as rebelling, and nothing much good results from it. However, you might want to take a closer look at the spiritual reality behind the faults. As discussed in chapter 5, are there patterns of fear, doubt, self-pity, jealousy, bitterness, hatred or besetting sins that have provided footholds in your organization's leadership for strongholds of demonic influence? Or has there perhaps been a history of arrogance, pride, self-promotion and self-centeredness? If so, what can be done about it?

Recognition of the enemy in the spiritual realm will be our starting place. The apostle Paul wrote about a spiritual reality that involves the structures that are needed to hold society together. He described spiritual powers—by a variety of names—that influence and infect organizational structures and the people who work within them. Paul identified the enemy, the real enemy of any organization: the *Powers*.[2]

We can utilize Scripture to arrive at several conclusions:

1. The Powers have several names: authorities, powers, rulers, thrones, dominions, principalities and sovereignties.
2. The form the Powers take is that of human prescriptions, traditions, rules and teachings, (and by inference, organizational purposes, policies, procedures and plans)— whatever structures that bring order, stability and regularity to the world and society and preserve them from chaos.
3. The Powers, as part of creation, are fallen. They claim for themselves the status of idols and demand unconditional loyalty, enslaving us and attempting to separate us from the love of Christ.
4. The Powers are the unseen enemy. We do not wrestle merely against flesh and blood. (As we struggle with poor leadership and fight for survival in dysfunctional organizations, we can be engaged in spiritual warfare and not even know it.)
5. The Powers have been exposed by Christ at the cross. Jewish law, the temple, piety and Roman justice—all posed as gods and were worshiped by the scribes, the priests, the Pharisees and Pilate, respectively. However, they were unmasked and shown to be false gods with the crucifixion of the one true God incarnate.
6. The Powers have been disarmed by Christ at the cross. Christ refused to be a slave to, or support the self-glorification of, any law, ideology, duty or philosophy; and in His death on the cross, He revealed Himself to be the ultimate provider of personal fulfillment and freedom from bondage.
7. The Powers must be dethroned. Their sovereignty must be broken by bringing them under the lordship of Jesus Christ.

These seven points about the Powers provide us with the framework for understanding the spiritual realities that make every organization a potential battlefield. If you choose to join the battle and fight for organizational change, you had better review these seven points thoroughly and often.

You might also take a moment to reflect on a few of the hang-ups that people have regarding the reality of the Powers and their effects, and whether any of those hang-ups apply to you. First, some of those who know something about the Powers believe that they did in fact exist at one time but that Christ totally destroyed them at the cross. What Christ actually did , however, was expose and disarm them at the cross and become the provision for their ultimate defeat.

Second, some would say that the only way to change an organization is to make sure a godly leader is in charge. The leader will make the necessary decisions to make the organization thoroughly Christian. Others would say that organizations don't hurt people, but that people do. So if all the individuals in the organization are Christian—if only Christians are hired—then it will be a Christian organization. Regrettably, in both of these views, the people are redeemed and brought under the lordship of Jesus Christ, but the Powers are not.

Third, there are folks who have a much narrower conception of spiritual warfare. They assume that if good operates through the individual, then so does evil. They believe, therefore, that the Powers are demons at work exclusively in and through individuals. This is a bias toward the individual, which modern society stresses and even the biblical view of salvation indirectly encourages. The additional biblical emphasis on structural evil as well as individual evil, unfortunately, is missed.

A fourth hang-up is the hankering or nostalgia for a previous time of security and direction under the simple and clear authority of a certain unifying idea or a particular kind of leader. Even though the idea or the leadership was inadequate or abusive before, this wishful thinking assumes that it will be better this time. Such thinking is like a dog returning to its vomit.[3]

You are now in the third phase of your recovery process, so you know who the enemy is. You have identified the Powers and know that they have become lords in their own right. They have demanded your loyalty to their neuroses, addictions or abusive practices, and they have wounded you deeply. According to the Dutch theologian, Hendrik Berkhof:

They have become gods (Galatians 4:8), behaving as though they were the ultimate ground of being, and demanding from men an appropriate worship. . . . They stand as a roadblock between the Creator and His creation.

They are "the rulers of this age" (I Corinthians 2:6). In their desire to rule they are in enmity toward the Lord of glory, who [will not] suffer them as lords.[4]

BIBLICAL GUIDELINES FOR ORGANIZATIONAL CHANGE

Using the biblical framework Paul has laid out for us, the question now is, how can the Powers be dethroned? Their sovereignty must be broken by bringing them under the lordship of Jesus Christ. We must redeem the Powers.

Again, Berkhof gives us perspective:

The Holy Spirit "shrinks" the Powers before the eye of faith. . . . The Nazis spoke of "nationhood," where the confessing church said "the nation" or preferably "the nations." In our Christian circles we would rather say "the authorities" than "the state." This is not so much because the two terms are not quite logically equivalent, as because of a wholesome intuition, seeing in "state" an autonomous power, whereas with "authorities" we think of ordinary men in higher positions. Where the Spirit of Christ rules, Mammon shrivels down to "finances". . . . Changing customs, slogans, and isms of the moment are seen as ideas which are merely "in the air," worth no more and no less than the older slogans they replaced. . . . Anxiety before the fearsome future gives way to a simple carefulness, since we know that the future as well is in God's hands.[5]

When "the Holy Spirit shrinks the Powers before the eye of faith," an organization's purpose converts from furthering its own kingdom to furthering God's kingdom. When the Spirit of Christ rules an organization's policies and procedures, they change from money-driven to ministry-driven. When an organization's business plans, marketing plans, strategic plans and contingency plans are in God's hands, complex schemes to secure the future become secondary to simple faith that knows ultimately all hope for the future is in God alone.

Redeeming the Powers in the life of an organization is a three-stage process, much like the recovery process in the life of an individual. It involves *discernment*, *de-deification* and *demonstration*, as suggested by Berkhof. These three stages correspond to recognition, remembrance and response, respectively.

Discerning is recognizing spiritual oppression by listening to the voice of God, so that you can speak the work of God. *De-deifying* is challenging the sovereignty of the Powers, by remembering that you have been liberated by Christ from putting your hope in the organization, its leader, mission or benefits. It is also remembering that nothing can separate you from the love of God in Christ Jesus. *Demonstrating* is responding in two ways: breaking demonic strongholds and changing the corporate culture in order to bring the organizational structures under the lordship of Jesus Christ. Let's consider each of these two ways of demonstrating.

Breaking the Strongholds

In chapter 5, we defined strongholds as entrenched patterns of thought, ideologies, values or behaviors that are contrary to the word and will of God. We saw how they operate in the individual's personality. Now we will look at how they operate in the organization's personality, or in other words, in the corporate culture.

Strongholds are evidence of Satan's activity in the structural life of the organization. They are not in themselves demons; they are instead the direct result of the unredeemed organization. They are the symptoms of the purposes, policies, procedures and plans that have not yet yielded to the lordship of Jesus Christ.

Your first step in breaking the strongholds is discerning their presence. There are a multitude of symptoms to look for. Following is a partial list of symptoms:[6]

1. Is there sin in the history of the organization that has not been dealt with? Old insults and improprieties that don't go away—that fester beneath the surface—have a palpably deadening effect on just about everyone in the organization.
2. Is there a pervasive feeling of mistrust poisoning the organization? Are people detached from one another, and uncommitted to the goals of the organization?
3. Is there a cloud of confusion hanging over the organization? Has the glory of the Lord seemed to have departed?
4. Is there divisiveness among the people? Are people developing their own little fiefdoms throughout the organization?
5. Is one person or group of persons dominating the functioning of the organization through a self-righteous, self-serving agenda?

Sin, mistrust, confusion, and personal fiefdoms and agendas are deadening. They produce an environment of detachment, divisiveness and domination from which the glory of the Lord has departed, and they can definitely be instruments of demonic influence. The biblical gifts of discernment and prophecy are essential in recognizing the situation for what it really is. It is also essential that the leadership of the organization listens to and heeds the warnings of those who have these gifts.

The second step is de-deifying the Powers. You do this by remembering that Christ has liberated you from having to put your hope in the things of this world, and that nothing the organization or the people in it do can separate you from the love of Christ. This simple act of faith puts the Powers in the right perspective and keeps structural evil from being lorded over you. Jesus—only Jesus—is Lord!

The third step is demonstrating the power of prayer. We should not think of prayer as just a weapon in our battle with the enemy. "Prayer isn't so much another weapon on our list of weaponry as it is the battle itself. It is the arena of conflict in which we engage our enemy."[7] Prayer is the supernatural arena for the battle. It is in prayer that we truly engage the demonic enemy.

Praying to break strongholds may be done both individually and corporately. If you have discerned the presence of strongholds in your organization, and if you have de-deified their lordship over you, then you are ready to go into battle. Use the following as your guide:

> The resistance to evil we feel is not itself "prayer." It is encounter, engagement, and enforcement of the divine will. We do not "pray" at the devil. We resist him with an authority that comes out of the prayer closet. And we defeat him with heavenly weapons. It is appropriate to remind the devil who he is and where he can go. Let me give you an example of this sort of statement: *I remind you, Satan, that Jesus came to destroy your works. I expose your work in this* [organization]. *I deny you further access and serve you notice that divine light is penetrating your darkness.... You are defeated. Jesus is Victor!*[8]

Your job is to rebuke the devil, not ream him out. It is not the force of your words that brings the victory, but the fact of the finished work on the cross.

I also recommend corporate prayer. You must do whatever you can to bring light to the darkness in every area possible. The Journey Wall Exercise provides a powerful opportunity to involve a group of believers in the breaking of strongholds through prayer.[9] This exercise can be used with any group that appropriately represents the organization, or the entire organization if it is small enough. The Journey Wall Exercise involves three basic steps.

Step one is the collection of information. Suggestions for the leader of the exercise are as follows:

1. Select a blank wall in the meeting room and tape easel paper onto it, one piece of paper for each five- or ten-year period of the organization's existence.
2. Ask each member of the group to think about significant people, events and circumstances from the organization's history and to write them down on a sheet of paper.

3. Break into small groups of five to seven and have individuals share what they wrote down. Ask each group to choose the most significant things that were shared and to record them on separate self-adhesive notes.
4. Have each group put its notes up on the wall, sticking them onto the appropriately dated pieces of easel paper. Ask them to circle each item that represents a painful situation.

Step two is prayerful intercession. Suggestions for the leader include the following:

1. Divide the small groups in half, and ask them to pray for God to speak to them. First, they should pray for God to reveal anything in themselves for which they should seek forgiveness, and second, they should pray for issues of hurt and reconciliation that have surfaced in the information collected during the exercise.
2. Gather the full group back together and ask each small group to report what God revealed to them. List the issues on an overhead projector, and allow time for any questions needed for clarification.
3. Spend time seeking the Lord in corporate prayer. Offer confession on behalf of the sins of "the forefathers," and pray for issues of discord that need to be confessed. Repent of individual and corporate sin—past and present—and openly ask for forgiveness and reconciliation with those who are present as well as absent.
4. Do not expect repentance for every sin and reconciliation of every relationship. Deal only with what the Lord shows you—do not push it. If some issue or issues cannot be resolved, decide what action needs to be taken at a later time. Then, if some of the pieces that are still currently broken are mended at that future time, perhaps the Journey Wall Exercise could be repeated to make the organization whole.

Step three is joyful inspiration. Suggestions for the leader include:

1. Remind the group that the biblical pattern is a time of repentance followed by a time of rejoicing. Try not to make too abrupt a transition. Offer them a break with refreshments and a time to tie up loose ends.
2. Reconvene in the original small groups. Have each group report the significant people, events and circumstances that they came up with earlier that were positive. List them on the overhead projector, and allow time for any questions needed for clarification.
3. Remind the group that God has been sovereignly at work in your organization, both in the past and in the present, in ways that have been hidden by the confusion and chaos created by the enemy. Ask each member to prayerfully consider each item on the list.
4. Invite the group to worship with praise and thanksgiving for what the Lord has done, what He is doing and what He will do. Celebrate His goodness together.

I believe that at least one other action is necessary in the breaking of corporate strongholds: to cleanse the physical property (buildings, rooms, offices) of any demonic presence:

> With your mature leaders, walk through your facility and claim each room for the Lord's glory. In prayer, apply the name and the blood of Jesus to remove the power of any enemy influence. Apply these prayers to specific rooms where offenses were known to have occurred.
>
> Ask God to break the power of any curses or demonic assaults that came against you during this time. Invite the Holy Spirit to fill and occupy your facility and to drive out anything unclean or evil.[10]

Many have done this, including myself, and have been blessed for having done it.

Changing the Culture

The culture of the organization is the *natural* arena for doing battle with the enemy. The corporate culture is the personality of the organization. It might also be called the character or even the soul, of the organization. The corporate culture is the site of spiritual warfare for the very soul of the organization. What better place to proclaim to the Powers that our God reigns?

Let's look at an operational definition of culture:

> Culture is defined as *shared* values, beliefs, expectations, attitudes, assumptions, and norms. These are seldom written down or discussed; rather, they are learned by living in the organization and becoming a part of it. . . .Culture fills in the gaps between what is formally decreed and what actually takes place. Culture thus determines how formal statements are interpreted and provides what written documents leave out.[11]

Corporate culture is comprised of the organization's relatively enduring values, beliefs, assumptions and norms. It is similar in definition to strongholds. Strongholds are evidence of Satan's activity at the structural level of the organization, and culture can give evidence to such activity as well. Both are symptomatic of purposes, policies, procedures and plans of the organization that do not function under the lordship of Jesus Christ. Therefore, the purposes, policies, procedures and plans are not carried out within a consistent biblical context, nor are they consistently critiqued with a biblical conscience. In other words, the organizational structures are not accountable to a biblical worldview—everything in every area of the organization is not viewed in relation to biblical values and beliefs, incarnated in Christ. Such values and beliefs would otherwise be the organization's guides for constructive thought and action.

When you break strongholds and change the culture, you create enormous pressure for structural change. For example, when leaders and workers alike are personally aligned with Christ, when there is repentance for corporate sin, and when the unwritten rules are accountable to a biblical worldview, then change is inevitable.

The people who create the written rules and who live by them will rewrite them to match who they are and what they are doing. They are following Christ, and He will show them the way.

The first thing you will want to do to begin changing the culture is to seek out someone in the organization with the gift of discernment, if you yourself do not have it. Discernment was the first of the three steps suggested earlier for breaking strongholds. This is an important first step, because you can easily be led by what you want to see rather than by what God wants you to see. Pray over your Change List, and ask the person with the gift of discernment to review it with you. Make any necessary changes to the list.

The second step is de-deifying the Powers. Again, you do this by remembering that Christ has liberated you from having to put your hope in the things of this world, and that nothing the organization or the people in it do can separate you from the love of Christ. You will need the support and encouragement of others to do that. You will need others who are in agreement with you and in whom you can trust. Who among your coworkers shares your concerns? Who among them thinks you are on the right track? Whom do you think will help you stay on track? Whom do you trust? It might be helpful for you to consider the types of coworkers you will run into as you begin to look for agreement and trust. I can think of five:[12]

1. **First, you will want to look for** *allies.* These are coworkers whom you can rate high on both agreement and trust. You will be able to talk with them about your doubts and dreams, about what's right and what's wrong, without fear that it will come back to haunt you. You will be able to be vulnerable and open, and you can expect the same in return. Allies will help you evaluate your perceptions and help you analyze the difficulties you will face.

2. **While looking for allies, you will find** *bedfellows.* These are folks who are high in agreement but low in trust. They will seem to be reacting to the same things you are, as far as you can see, and from what other people say. But, when you meet with them, they will seem to hold back. They will seem insecure and

self-protective. You won't quite trust them. Be a little careful about how much you share with them.

3. **You will also find** *fence sitters*—those who are unknown in agreement and low in trust. These people won't want to take a stand, one way or another. They will come across as patient and mature, but in actuality are primarily just cautious. They will speak of the need to bring grace into every area of conflict, but you will begin to wonder if that's God's agenda, or just their agenda.

4. **You will almost certainly find at least one or two** *opponents*. Interestingly, you will often discover them to be fairly high in trust, though they will obviously be low in agreement, since they oppose your view. Your disagreements with them will be straightforward, and you will know that you can have an honest discussion on the issues. If they are Christians, their Christian commitment will probably be as clear as yours, so it may be fruitful to negotiate on that basis with them, to see if you can reach agreement on the issues.

5. **Don't be surprised if you actually also find** *adversaries*. They are at the bottom of the pile: low in both agreement and trust. When you have an adversarial relationship, there is a problem that has gone beyond mere disagreement on the issues. Something has happened to sour the relationship. The person, for example, may be spreading untrue rumors about you, or actively undercutting you in conversations with your boss or pastor. I would not treat this as part of a culture-change agenda. It has become a personal issue and needs loving confrontation and forgiveness.

You will not be able to use adversaries to help you effect change. You can, however, use the other four types of coworkers. You will need to gather up support from those four types: your allies, those bedfellows and fence sitters who will support you in whatever way they can, and however many opponents you can persuade to join your cause. Then you will be ready to take your third step in changing the culture: demonstrating that the organizational structures are under the lordship of Jesus Christ.

I have had experience with several Christian organizations who wanted help in redeeming their organizational structures. They all adhered to basic Christian values, and their leaders and workers all were Christians. But something was deeply troubling about these organizations. Something was wrong with their personality. They were all soul-sick. Lots of energy was being expended in ways that didn't seem right for Christian organizations.

First Fruit Ministries (fictitious name) was one of those organizations, and I will summarize my work with them. We began with an analysis of the corporate culture and completed the process with a list of cultural characteristics that everyone agreed by consensus to use as goals. This became the basis for a complete review of First Fruit's purposes, policies, procedures and plans, in order to bring them under the lordship of Jesus Christ.

Everyone in the organization was asked to participate in a *Culture Survey*, a culture-evaluating exercise that indicated how energy was being expended throughout the organization. It also provided the basis for discussion of what First Fruit Ministries should look like in the future.[13] The Culture Survey consisted of open-ended questions that gave everyone the opportunity to anonymously put down in detail all the informal and formal values, standards of performance, expectations, assumptions, and pressures that they personally experienced while working at First Fruit. These were the questions on the Culture Survey:

1. List your perceptions of the *usual procedures and unwritten rules* that currently guide your attitude and behavior, and that affect what you bring to your job (e.g. it's okay to share personal information with your coworkers; document everything you do to make sure you get credit for it; don't complain).
2. Using one or two paragraphs, describe what to you would be the *ideal work environment*. In other words, what changes are needed? Include in your description how you would fit into your ideal, or what you would need to do to fit your own model.
3. Make a list of *new procedures and "rules"* that could govern your work activity and encourage discussion of difficult

and uncomfortable issues within your work group and within the organization as a whole.

The responses were first separated into two groups: *Actual* (what things need to be improved) and *Desired* (how things can be improved). They were then sorted into four culture-descriptive categories: *Task Support* (teamwork, sharing information, getting the job done), *Task Innovation* (creativity, rewards, self-improvement), *Social Relationships* (friendships, socializing on the job), and *Personal Freedom* (self-expression, being heard). The following tabulation shows the percentage of the Actual and Desired responses that fell into each of the four categories:

	Actual	Desired
• Task Support	42%	50%
• Task Innovation	22%	20%
• Social Relationships	0%	0%
• Personal Freedom	36%	30%

Analysis of these results revealed that the areas perceived as most in need of improvement were Task Support (teamwork) and Personal Freedom (self-expression). There was a secondary need in the area of Task Innovation (creativity). There was virtually no perceived need for improvement in the area of Social Relationships (friendships). These results were very indicative of a task-oriented, idealistic culture, which is often found in Christian organizations.

The contents of the individual responses showed energy being expended primarily around the issues of sharing information, getting the job done, and being heard. People were saying, "Care about us and communicate with us." "We are concerned about people-building and team-building." "We want to have input and the right to disagree."

They were asking for clear accountability, and equitable benefits and opportunities across all levels of the organization. They wanted a role in the decision-making process: giving input but not actually making the final decision, and getting feedback from the decision maker after a decision is made.

Several people brought up the issue of integrity—saying and doing the same thing. It was mentioned in connection with several problem areas: (a) making a promise and not carrying through, (b) having policies but not holding everyone to them, (c) saying we have participatory management but continuing top-down management, (d) encouraging employees to share their concerns but ignoring or penalizing them if the concerns appear negative, and (e) painting a picture of First Fruit Ministries to those outside the organization that does not accurately reflect reality.

This was clearly a work climate with lots of problems and a work force clamoring for solutions. A next step had to be taken to direct the strong desire for change into a process of discussion and commitment. Leaders and workers needed to sit down together to discuss a list of the problems as they saw them—openly and without fear of repercussion—and commit themselves to agreed-upon solutions.

A list was drawn up of the most frequently and clearly expressed complaints and recommended changes in the Culture Survey. The list totaled twenty-five items. Everyone was given a copy of the list, with the instructions: "Read and study each item, and ask yourself: (a) Does this make sense? (b) Are any modifications needed? and (c) Can I commit myself to it?"

A series of meetings was held, with everyone in the organization expected to attend. Everyone was encouraged to ask for clarification of each item as it was discussed and to suggest changes or to sign off on the item. They were also asked to bring each item under the scrutiny of Scripture, in order to ensure that no biblical principles were being violated.

The goal was consensus, which was defined as "I can live with it." Not everyone had to be in absolute agreement with every item, but no item could be accepted until everyone had declared that he or she could live with it. A final, revised list was then compiled that was agreed upon by consensus. That became the instrument for changing First Fruit's corporate culture. Here is the list that resulted:

VALUES

1. We value developing people within the context of achieving our tasks.
2. We value equitable benefits, rewards and opportunities for all employees.
3. We value employee input into the decision-making process.
4. We value dialogue that respects differing perspectives and opinions.
5. We value clearly communicated individual accountability within the organization.

INTENTIONS

1. We intend, as individuals accountable to the Lord, to show respect and appreciation for the dedication and contribution of every person at every level of the organization.
2. We intend that each supervisor and worker will verbally communicate on a regular basis, monthly or quarterly, as agreed upon by the work group.
3. We intend that each work group will meet at least weekly to share information and discuss departmental issues.
4. We intend to measure our effectiveness in terms of healthy staff relationships and task competency.
5. We intend to select managers who have a demonstrated capacity for enabling people as well as management and technical competence.
6. We intend that all new employees will receive orientation concerning standard operating procedures and expectations for employees.
7. We intend to develop, on an annual basis and wherever necessary, budgets and plans to improve staff performance.
8. We intend to promote from within whenever possible.
9. We intend that all policies and procedures—and their exceptions—will be equitably implemented throughout the organization.

10. We intend that work hours will be reasonable, clearly communicated and responsibly adhered to.
11. We intend that all appropriate staff, including managers, who are most directly and immediately affected by or involved in a course of action will meet to discuss it, and will conclude the meeting with a plan of action or designated time to continue the discussion if needed.
12. We intend that those who are affected by a decision will be informed of the outcome and its rationale in a timely fashion.
13. We intend in hiring situations that observations and perceptions will be solicited from the persons most directly affected by the position to be filled.
14. We intend that observations and perceptions will be solicited from the persons most directly affected by changes in departmental objectives, strategies or organization that are under consideration.
15. We intend that termination of employment, other than with cause and not related to organizational changes, will be done only after reasonable and clearly communicated evaluation of performance and appropriate attempts to facilitate improvement.
16. We intend that disagreements will be viewed as reasons for honest dialogue, not strategies for creating dissension.
17. We intend that questions, observations and instructions will be sincerely listened to, honestly answered, and followed up on in good faith.

This is truly an inspired list of commitments. You can do something similar in your organization. Just follow these guidelines:

1. Identify your allies and any others who can support your cause and agree to follow this course of action.
2. Secure permission from the leadership to proceed.

3. Distribute the Culture Survey, with its three open-ended questions, to everyone in the organization. Remember, participation is anonymous.

4. Include the items on your Change List in your own responses to the survey.

5. Select someone (perhaps an outside consultant) to collect the surveys and tally the responses. The responses should be summarized in a list of the most frequently and clearly expressed complaints and recommended changes. The list can total anywhere from ten to twenty-five items. It is not necessary to do the cultural analysis with the four culture-descriptive categories.

6. Give everyone a copy of the list, with instructions to ask the following questions about each item: Does this make sense? Are any modifications needed? Can I commit myself to it? Does it square with Scripture?

7. Arrange for a series of meetings to discuss the items. Attendance should be mandatory for everyone in the organization. Again, permission must be granted by the leadership, who must agree to attend all the meetings themselves and to not penalize anyone for anything that is said.

8. Appoint a facilitator (again, perhaps an outside consultant). You may need more than one group, depending on the size of the organization and the ability of the facilitator. Group size may vary from ten to twenty members. The appointed facilitator should conduct every meeting of every group.

    The job of the facilitator is to keep the meetings on track and within agreed-upon time limits, to ensure that everyone gets an opportunity to voice an opinion about every item, and to prevent anyone from dominating the discussion. The facilitator will also need to move the discussion on to the next item when agreement cannot be reached, and to revise the list of items for each meeting based on the previous meeting's discussion.

9. Instruct the facilitator to compile a final list of agreed-upon items after the original list has been discussed to everyone's satisfaction. A final meeting should be held to formally adopt—by consensus—your organization's commitments and expectations for the future.

10. Ask everyone to agree to be mutually accountable to what has been agreed upon by consensus. In addition, establish a grievance procedure, in order to hold those who do not keep their word responsible for their actions.

May the Lord richly bless your efforts. May the Holy Spirit blow over the strongholds, blow through the structures, and bring new life to your organization where there was sin and stagnation. And may the Lord build His organization, as you stand with Him, and as you stand against the Powers of Satan.

Moving On

PICTURE A STORM. Storm clouds on the horizon. Winds picking up. Your barometer says a storm is brewing. Suddenly you see lightning and hear thunder far off. Then closer. The rain begins. It becomes torrential. Now lightning is flashing and thunder is crashing almost overhead. Soon it passes, and you wonder: Is there going to be a rainbow? Is there going to be flooding?

How are you weathering your storm? You knew it was coming, but you couldn't really prevent it. Perhaps you've thought of abiding—riding out the storm—much like enduring the steady rain. Or perhaps changing things has been in your thoughts: "I could create some thunder and lightning of my own. That would wake them up and make them take notice. Get the wind of change blowing through this place."

Maybe you're thinking about quitting. If so, you're probably wondering what it will bring. Will it be a rainbow, an outward testimony to the sunshine of hope within you? Or will it be the avoidance of being submerged in a flood of hopelessness? Quitting seems universally to have those two poles. Looked at on the bright side, as a rainbow, quitting is a matter of principle, a reflection of your finest values and a resplendent display of taking a stand for what is right and honorable. Looked at on the darker side, as avoidance of a flood, quitting is a matter of self-preservation. You simply have to head for higher ground, or you will be immersed in your wounds and drown.

Whether you quit on principle or for self-preservation, you are choosing the most deeply emotional of the three choices for responding to your personal storm. "I quit" are two words that can shake you to the core.

SHOULD YOU LEAVE?

Considering the magnitude of the decision, how do you know if you should stay or leave? Look back at your Organization Test results from chapters 3–5. Which of the three response categories captured the bulk of your experience? Were your responses primarily in the *Sometimes* and *Never* categories, and adverse things happen infrequently enough that you can stick with it and minister to others? Or do adverse things happen with enough frequency that you must confront them and make changes? Perhaps, though, your responses were primarily in the *Always* category, and adverse things happen so frequently that you have to face it and move on.

If you do not feel you are being forced to leave, you may want to try to make some changes in the system to make life more livable. However, do not be too surprised if you find that the chances of success are very slim. The nature of organizations defies change. Even so, I encourage you to try. But what if the leadership won't let you distribute a Culture Survey and arrange for meetings to arrive at consensus for committing to changing the culture? What if they won't listen to discernment concerning the presence of strongholds or let you initiate the Journey Wall Exercise for breaking the strongholds? Your options in that case are to either keep on (abide and pray for divine intervention) or move on.

Whatever your situation might be, you definitely should consider speaking up before giving up. Give voice to your concerns about un-Christlike behavior, and speak the truth in love when you see injustice wounding God's people. Then, if your words of truth and compassion fall on deaf ears, you may just have to shake the dust off your feet and let them look after their own house. As it says in the Old Testament, "When all Israel saw that the king refused to listen to them, they answered the king: 'What share do we have in David, what part in Jesse's son? To your tents, O Israel! Look after your own house, O David!' "[1] And in the New Testament, we are told, "If anyone will not welcome you or listen to your words, shake the dust off your feet when you leave . . . ."[2]

EXIT AND VOICE

Have you spoken up and been burned or been blown off? Have you decided that it is a lost cause? Have you decided to leave the organization and let them look after their own house? If so, you are now faced with another difficult decision. It is round two of speaking up: letting people know exactly why you are leaving. This will be one of the most vividly tense times in your entire work history. You will want so badly to vent your indignation, yet there will be few, if any, opportunities to do so.

Indignation comes in two varieties: righteous and self-righteous. Either way, you want to cry out, as well as get out. If it is righteous indignation, you feel driven, if not to preserve your own honor, then to prevent the ongoing abuse of others, to blow the whistle, and to make things right. If it is self-righteous indignation, you feel driven to get even. However, getting even— self-promotion at someone else's expense—is never right. Therefore, if you want to exit and speak up—to have a voice— then do so out of righteous indignation, not *self*-righteous indignation.

Up to this point, your voice has been all inside your own head, and it's confusing. You may be telling yourself that your reason for leaving is to focus everyone's thoughts on the issues, so that something will finally change. Or, perhaps you self-righteously think that it would be a severe blow to the organization and a wonderful way for you to show them a thing or two. Maybe you're even thinking that if you simply threaten to resign, it will shape them up or ensure a better future for yourself.

Don't kid yourself. I have never met the person who was right when he or she was convinced that an actual or threatened exit would be a catalyst for change, a crushing blow to the organization, or a successful source of leverage for the future. Your feelings and thoughts are all normal, but you will need a better reason for your exit. You will also need to understand the interplay between exiting and having a voice, and how one affects the other.[3]

Actual exit, the act of leaving, is clear cut and either-or. Having a voice, however, is rarely, if ever, clear cut and evolves in many directions at once. Therefore, as the opportunity for exit gets stronger, the opportunity for voice gets weaker. Conversely, in organizations where exit is not likely, voice is much more viable. For example, exit from the overall body of Christ is rare, even though changing church memberships is relatively easy. You may exit the particular church you're attending, but you will not exit the larger body of Christ. Instead, you will typically begin to voice your opinion regarding the Church. Ironically, people usually leave their church without much of a fuss (although there certainly are exceptions), but most will then have a lot to say—some will even write a book—about the Church, and how it can be improved.

Another thing to consider as you prepare your voice is that those who care the most about the quality of the organization tend to exit when the organization begins to deteriorate. In contrast, those who care the least will exit when demands for quality increase. When the quality of an organization deteriorates and people are being wounded, that's when those who care the most will leave— the emotional cost has gotten too high. But, when demands for quality increase along with the accompanying need to work harder to increase quality, that's when those who care the least will leave— the energy cost has gotten too high.

Loyalty

A factor that works to counterbalance the early exit of those who care the most is their *loyalty*. It is enormously important to note that loyalty contains within it a strong dose of expectation that something or someone will change:

As a rule . . . loyalty holds exit at bay and activates voice. It is true that, in the face of discontent with the way things are going in an organization, an individual member can remain loyal without being influential himself, but hardly without the expectation that *someone* will act or *something* will happen to improve matters.[4]

True loyalty is belief in the ideal of the very best that the organization can possibly be. It is holding on to the ideal, hoping that it will happen. This is a powerful antidote to the previously mentioned tendency of those who care the most about the quality of the organization to exit when things begin to deteriorate. Loyalty will hold them longer. When we define loyalty this way, it also blows away that old line, "If you complain, you're being disloyal." Haven't you heard that before? What a control device!

While we are on the subject of loyalty, let me say a few words about *disloyalty*. Dysfunctional organizations are based on misplaced loyalties. Loyalty in these organizations is expressed in terms of loyalty to the company or church, loyalty to the boss or pastor, or even loyalty to one's country. Disloyalty is seen as taking a stand for individual rights, rather than just "going along" for the corporate good. Or it is seen as taking a side that differs from the boss's or pastor's on an issue. It is even seen as taking exception to the statement: "My country, right or wrong. Love it or leave it." This is not, however, the understanding of disloyalty that I would like to convey.

My understanding of disloyalty is that it is giving up on your belief in the best that your organization or leadership can be. It is giving up on any expectation of positive change. Disloyalty is being faithful to the organization and leadership as they are, rather than to what and to whom they can become. Voicing one's opinion or taking a stand, with fidelity to the best that can be, is not disloyalty. Keeping silent, giving up and leaving—that's disloyalty.

Disloyalty is not in the voice. It is in the exit. I point this out because the accusation of disloyalty carries with it a real sting.

Don't be derailed when you are voicing your concerns and someone accuses you of being disloyal. No, instead, you are actually being loyal: loyal to God's vision, purpose and design for the organization. If, after your determined and resourceful use of your opportunity for voice, the organization proves that it will not consider the ideal and work toward it in some positive fashion, and you exit, then you can be considered to be disloyal. However, you are not being disloyal to the organization, per se, or to its leader. Rather, you are being disloyal to a hopeless situation, where there is no expectation of constructive change, and this is a proper kind of disloyalty.

Perhaps you are thinking, "I don't want to be disloyal to a hopeless situation, because things will only get worse if I leave." You may believe this to be true, but I have my doubts. I believe the situation will probably get worse even if you stay. If exit is a serious option, then your exercise of the voice option has undoubtedly not been effective up to this point. Why should that change in the future?

Perhaps you also believe that if you exit and tell the truth as to why, you will do the organization unjustified harm. I believe that this is also misguided. Although I have stated that the hope of exit being a catalyst for change is not generally valid, there is an exception. If you determine that some influential people still remain in the organization who care about the ideal, then if you resign and go public with your protest, you might actually do a lot of good. "The jolt provoked by clamorous exit of a respected member is in many situations an indispensable complement to voice."[5] In such a situation, your exit can encourage the voice of others, but it may never happen if you fail to exercise your opportunity for voice and just go quietly.

There are two steps that should help you at this juncture. First, determine how loyalty is defined in your organization. If it equals blind faith in the leadership or organizational policies, exit without voice is probably your better option. You can recognize blind-faith loyalty when leaders say, "Just trust me," yet they have not proven themselves to be trustworthy. Blind-faith loyalty is also at work when you are told, "Don't question how we do things around here. God has brought us through difficult times, and there's no reason to change now."

Second, determine how many of the people who remain in the organization care deeply about the quality of the organization. If most of those have left and the few who remain are not particularly influential in the organization, then how will the organization reform itself from within? Exit without voice is, again, probably the better option.

EXIT STRATEGY

When should you exit, and how should you exit? These are the two tough questions that must be answered. You must not merely stumble into, or back into, your departure. Don't just give up and go. Departing should not be by default. The Lord must be directing you in when and how to move on, just as He would need to be directing you in how to minister to others, or to make changes. Your moving on must involve just as much strategy. Therefore, we will look next at the two primary components of moving on, which you will use to build a successful exit strategy: the matter of *timing* and the method of *leave-taking*.

Timing

The chairman and president of the largest human resource management consulting firm in the world have found seven danger signs that should alert people that it is time to seriously consider leaving a job:[6]

1. *You hate your job.* Be honest with yourself. Call it for what it is.
2. *You lose your voice.* Again, be honest. Have coworkers stopped communicating with you? Are you being excluded from important meetings and not being considered for challenging assignments?
3. *You get negative feedback.* Don't let positive stuff, like a personal friendship with the boss, obscure negative feedback

about performance. Sooner or later it will catch up with you.
4. *The economy is working against you.* Is your job becoming obsolete? Is the company in financial trouble?
5. *You're not personally productive.* You're just muddling through. You've lost your motivation to do the job.
6. *You miss objectives.* You're motivated in the wrong areas. You're compensating for loss of job interest with heavy involvement in areas that are not really part of your job description.
7. *You fail to change.* Are you becoming obsolete? Are you so stuck in your ways that you refuse to grow with the company?

These are clicks on the clock. They are timers. They are seven minutes on a time bomb that's waiting to go off in ten minutes. You know what's wrong with the organization, and you know how you have been wounded emotionally. You also know how you're doing on the job itself. What more do you need?
Let me put it a bit more eloquently:

Work is love made visible.
And if you cannot work with love but only with distaste, it is better that you should leave your work and sit at the gate of the temple and take alms of those who work with joy.
For if you bake bread with indifference, you bake a bitter bread that feeds but half man's hunger.
And if you grudge the crushing of the grapes, your grudge distils a poison in the wine.
And if you sing though as angels, and love not the singing, you muffle man's ears to the voices of the day and the voices of the night.[7]

If you hate your work, you will plant bitterness in others' hearts and poison the fruits of your labors. And if you refuse to exit, you will muffle the voice of others who could bring about positive change, if only they could be heard.

So, what about leaving your church? Again, you know what's wrong with the organization, and you know how you have been wounded emotionally. Let's look at those seven danger signs one more time—with slight modification—to see how you're actually functioning in the life of the church.

1. *You dislike going to church.* You look for excuses not to go. When you get there, you're bored, and when you leave, you're angry.
2. *You lose your voice.* Other members and even the leadership don't respond when you have been absent. They don't respond to you when you are there, either, and they don't include you in areas where you could be a helpful resource.
3. *You get negative feedback.* Some folks in the church have mentioned your lack of contribution to the work of the church. They are speaking the truth in love, and they are right.
4. *The trends for the future are working against you.* Is your giftedness out of place? Is your church dying?
5. *You're not personally productive.* You're spiritually flat, or perhaps you're burned out. You're not participating in any ministry of the church.
6. *You miss opportunities.* You're not motivated to respond to new ministry needs. You're not praying for God to reveal any to you, either.
7. *You fail to change.* When something good happens in your church, do you refuse to acknowledge it? Are you not growing with your church as, in spite of its difficulties, it moves forward?

What about leaving a spiritually abusive church? Here are eleven helpful guidelines:[8]

1. *Does grace have a chance?* Can God turn it around? If the leadership is power-posturing, performance-preoccupied and evidently permanent, the answer is probably not.

2. *Are you supporting what you hate?* Why?

3. *Do you need to be right?* Are you frustrated by the question, "If I'm right about what's wrong around here, why should I be the one to leave?"

4. *Can you stay, and stay healthy, both at the same time?*

5. *Can you decide your own limits—and stick with them?*

6. *Can you accept that God cares more about the church than you do?* Or are you hung up with the question, "Will they ever really know what's going on?"

7. *Is it possible that the system might need to die?* "Leaving does not kill a dead system, it just makes it look as dead as it is. There are times God writes *Ichabod,* 'the glory of the Lord has departed,' on the door and leaves."[9]

8. *Are you trying to help the system, even though you are exhausted?* Good luck.

9. *Are you able to listen to the voice of sanity?* Seek the counsel of mature Christians outside the system.

10. *Do you know where to sow?* Remember the parable of the sower and the seed!

11. *If you came today for the first time, knowing what you now know about the system, would you stay?* Enough said.

Leave-Taking

Now that you have decided when to leave, there is still much left to be done. You need to decide how to leave. To complete your exit strategy, you must go through five doors.

1. Control your obsession with your pain. You will get nowhere if you continue to make your wound your dwelling place, rather than recognizing it as the disguise that it really is. Continuing to dwell in your wound will control everything else you do. Instead, look at your wound for what it really is. It is your emotional response to a crazy situation. It is not your response to a normal situation, nor is it you. You are more than your wound. It is only a disguise.

The most common emotional disguise is *anger.* Anger is used to hide all kinds of other emotions. When you can't pinpoint what it is that is bothering you, anger will cover it nicely. Take guilt, for example. In most Christian organizations the power of the promise, the grandiose nature of the mission, and the very fact that it is a Christian organization make it really hard to fold up your tent and just walk away. Guilt, or even shame, is the usual response that you will feel. But your anger will hide your other negative emotions, even from yourself, and make leave-taking that much easier. I wonder: Is that why it is so common for Christians, when they are fired or when they quit on their own, to work themselves up to an intense level of anger—almost hate—toward the organization or someone in it? Is it a disguise of guilt because of feelings of having failed God or of having let Him down?

You can take control of your own responses. Other people cannot hurt you, unless you let them. You do not need to let your wound control you. Here's an example, given by organizational consultants who have worked with people wounded by addictive organizations:

> We have worked with scores of people who are casualties of addictive organizations. Inevitably, they are some of the brightest and most highly motivated men and women. They are the ones who stretch themselves, maximize learning, and devote time and energy to their company. However, many of them are leaving. They report that over time, they saw they were in companies that were addictive environments and therefore destructive. The companies implicitly asked the employees to remain blind to what they were seeing . . . . [The dysfunctional actions of the companies] left these employees with a sense of moral exhaustion and deterioration. For the most part, they decided *they could not change the company by themselves, but they could take responsibility for their own lives.* Most left the organization [emphasis mine].[10]

The same applies to abusive organizations:

> Moving on from abusive experiences requires the realization that *one can take control over the feelings of abuse and the responses of*

wounding. One need not repeat the abuses or responses of the past. It is common . . . to blame other individuals and the system for the abuse that was perpetrated. Though others were responsible for the abusive events, [one] must come to see how [he or] she has participated in the wounding process by responding to abusive events with wounds of self-denial and self-devaluation. To attribute the whole process to others gives them power over the self—the power to abuse and wound.

   To take back control, the individual must take back the power of controlling [his or] her response. [He or] she must choose a healing response to an abusive event. [He or] she must take responsibility for the creation of [his or] her future self [emphases mine].[11]

Give yourself time to recuperate from your moral exhaustion and to recover from your massive denial of self. Don't quit on the spot. Don't delude yourself by thinking that you'll get even by quitting right then and there. "Get mad, but don't get even; get *ahead.*"[12]

   2. Consider your obligations. Most career specialists advise lining up another job before leaving your present one, since your financial obligations must still be met. You need to know whether there is a job for you, and if there is, whether it will be adequate for you to meet your financial commitments.

   Will you be able to cover the necessities? Will you be able to pay the mortgage and other debt payments? Will you lose your medical coverage? What about life insurance and disability insurance? What about your retirement plan, if you have one? Your financial priorities are just as much a part of the decision-making process as is gaining control over your obsession with your pain.

   3. Consider your options. There have been many books written by career specialists that will help you develop action plans and a career plan.[13] Some typical areas that they cover are clarifying your values and interests, discovering your abilities (and in Christian publications, your spiritual gifts), researching job opportunities, drawing up a career plan, writing a résumé, and interviewing for the job. Each book will take you through these areas step by step and will guide you toward options that are right for you.

I would strongly encourage you to put a spiritual foundation under any effort that you put into considering your options. First, identify specific times in the past when God has clearly guided you. These are called *spiritual markers*, and they will help you to see God's perspective of your past and present.[14] When your markers align with an option for the future, they will give you confidence in the path you should take. However, when there is no consistency with any option for the future, God may be telling you to continue praying and seeking His guidance.

An effective way to identify spiritual markers is the Time-Line Exercise.[15] This will help you to see how God has been at work in your life, perhaps in ways that you have not previously recognized. Start by writing down the significant people, events and circumstances that have shaped your life throughout your life history. Organize them chronologically and note those that represent painful or negative experiences. Next, list insights that you have gained from those items: insights that you believe God has used in shaping your life into what it is today. Pay particular attention to transition times, times when you were encountering change, considering making a commitment, or coping with a crisis. These insights that God has shown you—through times of change, commitment and crisis—are your spiritual markers for your present circumstance. Identifying these markers is the first step in forming your spiritual foundation.

A second step in establishing your spiritual foundation is to develop a personal *mission statement*. This involves bringing together three things: the Bible verses that give a biblical framework for your life, your core values, and your vision for the future.[16] Writing a personal mission statement will be especially enlightening for you if you have made the same error that many people do: adopting the organization's mission statement as your personal one. If you have made this error, it will be well worth your while to carefully develop a personal mission statement—do not simply personalize a corporate mission statement and attempt to use it as an aid in determining your future.

To develop a personal mission statement, you will need to follow several steps. Start by listing those Bible verses that most clearly define your purpose in life. Select enough verses to cover the most important areas of your life. For example, what do you want to be like—how do you desire to emulate Christ at home, at work, in relationships, in the allocation and consumption of resources, and in thought as well as deed? Next, list the values that express your most deeply held convictions and biblical principles, the values that have shaped your character.

Turning your attention to the future, write down what you believe is God's preferred future for you, or in other words, your personal vision. Incorporate responses to these questions: What is your ministry passion? What does God want you to accomplish to further His kingdom? What is your destiny? Finally, blend together the verses, values and vision that God has given you, forming a summation statement that touches the most important areas of your life. This is your personal mission statement.

4. **Consult your family and friends.** Bring everything you have accumulated so far—your pain, your financial priorities and your plans—to the doorsteps of your family and friends. However, don't just "dump and run." You have a lot to share with them, but you also have a lot to hear from them. Make sure you carefully consider their input.

Ask your spouse: "How is the Holy Spirit leading you, independently of how He may be leading me, regarding where we should live, how we should live, and what each of us should be doing?" Discuss with your children how a move would affect their schooling and friendships. Ask your friends who know you best to be bluntly honest with you. And *pray* together as a family. Ask your friends to pray for you. Not just once but until the Lord gives you peace. Prayer is the pivotal point of the entire process.

5. **Carefully plan your departure.** Because of all the work that's involved before you actually go out the door, I believe that your departure should be carried out gradually, rather than abruptly. Here's how a friend of mine, who found that he could no longer remain on the pastoral staff of his church, put it:

First, I tried to "not need" relationships with the other staff members. I began to disengage, to let things slide. Like unwillingness to confront problems anymore, or even speak candidly when others brought them up. I began to no longer care about the organization.

I needed to disengage and distance myself mentally and emotionally. It allowed me to leave gradually and gracefully.

Notice that he let caring and confronting slide. But he did not let his competence on the job slide. If he had, he would have been fired before he had a chance to quit!

When you leave, there are two ways to depart: loudly or quietly. Both, with effort, can be done gracefully. If everyone else who cares deeply about the quality of the organization has already left, then a quiet departure is better than a loud one. There is no other voice for change, so nothing you say will make any difference. In the special case where many who remain are exercising their collective voice in rebellion, a quiet departure will also protect you from the self-aggrandizing temptation to lead the rebellion. Consider the following:

> In the spiritual realm, a man who will lead a rebellion has already proven, no matter how grandiose his words or angelic his ways, that he has a critical nature, an unprincipled character, and hidden motives in his heart. Frankly, he is a thief. He [multiplies] dissatisfaction and tension within the realm, and then either seizes power or siphons off followers.[17]

Being a thief and siphoning off followers is not Christlike. "There's only *one* way to leave . . . *Alone*. All alone."[18]

However, you can also be deceived in the calm just as easily as in the commotion. It is true that a quiet departure may keep you from leading a rebellion for self-gain and from making acrimonious parting gestures. However, it may also deeply implicate you in the very thing that you are trying to oppose by leaving. People may think that if you don't speak up, you have acquiesced and must support it. Actually, the errors of aggrandizement, acrimony and acquiescence are all in the same boat. You don't want to be in that boat.

A loud departure may therefore at times be the more effective and honest way to go. The distinguished organizational psychologist, Warren Bennis, puts it succinctly:

> The garden-variety resignation is an innocuous act, no matter how righteously indignant the individual who tenders it. The act is made innocuous by a set of organization-serving conventions that few resignees are able (or, for a variety of personal reasons, even willing) to break. When the properly socialized dissenter resigns, he or she tiptoes out. [The news is released] on the letterhead of the departing one's superior. "I today accepted with regret the resignation of . . .," it reads. The pro forma statement rings pure tin in the discerning ear, but this is the accepted ritual nonetheless. One retreats under a canopy of smiles, with verbal bouquets and exchanges, however insincere, of mutual respect. *The last official duty of the departing one is to keep his or her mouth shut. The rules of play require that the last word goes to those who remain inside* [emphasis mine].[19]

A quiet departure can be an empty gesture just as easily as a loud departure can be a wrathful gesture. Conversely, a loud departure can be graceful to the same extent that a quiet departure can be meaningful. But it is not easy to execute a loud departure gracefully.

If you have exercised common Christian graces up to this point, however, the quality of your exit will probably hinge on how you write the letter. You will need to write something to someone to make your resignation official. In doing so, there are certain guidelines you should follow. State simply that you are resigning and when your resignation will be effective. Include any plans that you have made for a smooth transition. Finally, conclude with a positive statement about your time with the organization. You do not need to list your reasons for leaving or to state your plans for the future. That can be done in face-to-face meetings with those who ask.

If part of your agenda is to leave the door partway open for the possibility of returning to the organization sometime in the future, and if you have not been overly critical up to this point, you should be okay. However, what if your agenda is to reveal critical information that you believe can be used constructively to improve the organization but that you know will not get past your boss unless you reveal it yourself? Now we're talking about a second kind of letter—the *real* letter.

In every organization in which I have ever worked, I have counseled people who have been determined to write that second kind of letter—usually to the board and usually loaded with anger. It was almost their entire focus, their entire exit strategy. They had not yet even gone through Door One of the leave-taking process, and here they were knocking on Door Five. My advice to them was to write the letter out in detail, with no holds barred. Then, throw the letter away. Do not send it. Write it again later—four doors later—and then send it.

If you are now at the point of writing a letter to the board as the final step of your exit strategy, remember the following:

> One looks for things to be said in letters that are not said elsewhere, expecting truth most of all. Even falsity in letters divulges a kind of truth—the false wit employed in writing to a clever enemy, the false cheer to a dull friend, the false authority to children, the false self-confidence to colleagues. Letters conceal almost nothing, which accounts for their power.[20]

Leave aside all of your falsities. Speak only the truth in love. Have it critiqued by your most trusted friends. Inform your boss of your letter, and send him or her a copy. And release it totally to God.

I have one more thing to say about graceful leave-taking: Remember those you leave behind. Make sure that in both the timing and the execution of your exit strategy, your main accomplishment is not to simply add to their burden. In addition, be sure to pray for them after you have left.

Epilogue

G OD SPEAKS THROUGH GODLY PEOPLE regardless of their pain or position. Wounds are a weapon of the enemy, however, to turn ears away from God and to silence His voice amongst His people. An important part of your recovery process is to hear the voice of God, so that you can speak the word of God. Your place of work or worship needs your witness to the truth, and the Powers who think they rule your organization need to see that they don't actually rule it—Jesus does.

I have found that, with few exceptions, hearing from God concerning the organization's future is "easier" than hearing from Him regarding one's own future. I have known countless Christian workers who could put their finger on the pulse of the irregular heartbeat of their organization and in some cases also pinpoint the exact cause with uncanny accuracy. Some have even received visions of the glory of the Lord departing. With regard to their own future, however, most of these people didn't have a clue.

I recently left a job where this certainly was the case. While on the job, I was able to discern corporate realities and offer a prophetic voice on a fairly consistent basis. However, I found it much more difficult to discern God's leading for my personal future if I were to leave. Consequently, my leave-taking was in a sort of limbo for an extended period of time. There was too much "noise" to hear

God's voice at a personal level. Too much corporate pressure for planning and not enough praying—both for the future of the ministry and for my place in it. I needed to stop laboring in vain and start listening to the voice of God. I needed to turn away from diversion in order to find direction.

That's when God spoke to me: "And He brought us out from there in order to bring us in."[1] I realized that I first had to leave, so that God could then show me where He was leading me. So, from the impact of perceiving corporate realities and by the impulse of the Holy Spirit, I became sure of my departure, although not sure of my destination. I was not certain where I was going, but I was very certain that God would be my guide.

Does the Lord want to bring you out of your present situation, so that He can lead you into another situation that is more suited to His purpose? Or, instead, is He leaving you where you are for a purpose? Either way, let Him be your guide. Let Him speak to your heart: "Do not use your freedom as an opportunity for the flesh, but through love be servants of one another."[2] He would not have you to use your present situation as an opportunity for the flesh—for vindictive complaining if you stay, or for a vengeful farewell if you choose to leave. In other words, do not inflict wounds on the body of Christ, but rather forgive wrongs and reconcile relationships wherever possible.

Let me remind you of an earlier warning given in chapter 10 regarding people with rebellion in their heart. In spite of their high-sounding pontifications and self-righteous accusations, in reality they are only thieves. They cause dissension and dissatisfaction, and they loot and plunder material and human resources for their own purposes. They do not further the kingdom of God but only their own. They are bitter about their circumstance and blame God for not making it better. They sneeringly demand (like the thief alongside Christ on the cross, as depicted in chapter 2), "Aren't you the Christ? Save me!"

Therefore, do not speak with a *vitriolic* voice, but with a *victorious* voice. You have already won the victory, in the Lord Jesus Christ. Do not have revenge in your heart. Do not throw spears, even though King Saul's spear has pierced your own heart. You do not need someone else to pay the price for your wounds. Jesus has paid the price—the only price that you need in order to forgive, and in order to let Him be your guide.

Let God speak to you through the following words from Romans 12. The notations indicate the Bible versions used from the list at the end. Let His voice guide your voice as you come before Him in prayer and promise—as you seek to please Him in all that you do.

Pray to Heed God's Voice

- Don't become so well adjusted to your culture that you fit into it without even thinking.*
- Be transformed by the renewing of your mind. Then you will be able to test and approve what God's will is—his good, pleasing and perfect will.†
- Do not be conceited or think too highly of yourself.§
- Don't burn out; keep yourselves fueled and aflame.*
- Don't quit in hard times; pray all the harder.*
- If a man's gift is prophesying, let him use it in proportion to his faith.† If you help, just help, don't take over; if you teach, stick to your teaching; if you give encouraging guidance, be careful that you don't get bossy; if you're put in charge, don't manipulate.* If you are helping others in distress, do it cheerfully.§
- Practice hospitality.†
- Don't be stuck-up. Make friends with nobodies; don't be the great somebody.*
- Live in harmony with one another.†
- Rejoice with those who rejoice; mourn with those who mourn.†

Promise to Heed God's Voice

- Offer yourselves as living sacrifices, holy and pleasing to God.†

- Honor one another above yourselves.[†]
- As far as it depends on you, live at peace with everyone.[†]
- Be joyful in hope, patient in affliction, faithful in prayer.[†]
- Love in all sincerity, loathing evil and clinging to the good.[§]
- Bless your enemies; no cursing under your breath.[*]
- Never pay back evil for evil.[§]
- Do not seek revenge, but leave a place for divine retribution; for there is a text which reads, "Justice is mine, says the Lord, I will repay."[§]
- If you see your enemy hungry, go buy that person lunch, or if he's thirsty, get him a drink.[*]
- Do not be overcome by evil, but overcome evil with good.[†]

To God be the glory! Amen.

---

[*]   From The Message.
[†]   From the New International Version.
[§]   From the New English Bible.

NOTES

INTRODUCTION

1. See Hosea 8:7.
2. See Jeremiah 29.11.
3. *Christianity Today* (1993). "Personnel Woes Persist at Larson Ministries,"September 13, p. 62.
4. See Hart, A. D. (1993). *The Crazy-Making Workplace*. Ann Arbor, MI: Servant.
5. See White, W. L. (1986). *Incest in the Organizational Family: The Ecology of Burnout in Closed Systems*. Bloomington, IL: Lighthouse Training Institute.

ONE
Words of the Wounded

1. An excellent resource is Christians for Biblical Equality, 122 W. Franklin Avenue, Suite 218, Minneapolis, MN, 55404-2451.
2. The italicized terminology was inspired by Heatherley, J. L. (1987). *Unworld People*. New York: HarperCollins.
3. A helpful resource for assessing the risks and successfully raising concerns is Ryan, K. D., Oestreich, D. K., & Orr, G. III. (1996). *The Courageous Messenger: How to Successfully Speak Up at Work*. San Francisco: Jossey-Bass.
4. See Ryan, K. D., & Oestreich, D. K. (1991). *Driving Fear Out of the Workplace: How to Overcome the Invisible Barriers to Quality, Productivity, and Innovation*. San Francisco: Jossey-Bass.

5. *Chicago Tribune* (1979). "Wife's Feminism Costs Bible Professor His Job: Theology School Casts Out a Feminist," September 9, pp. 1, 5.
6. I am indebted for the discussion of loss of credibility to Kathleen Ryan and Daniel Oestreich.
7. Lewis, C. S. (1947). *The Abolition of Man*. New York: Macmillan. P. 35.
8. See Reich, R. B. (1987). "Entrepreneurship Reconsidered: The Team as Hero." *Harvard Business Review*, 65 (3), pp. 77–83.
9. See Bennis, W. (1989). *Why Leaders Can't Lead: The Unconscious Conspiracy Continues*. San Francisco: Jossey-Bass.
10. Psalm 137:1–4, The Living Bible.
11. Heatherley, p. 33.

TWO
Guidelines for Recovery

1. Genesis 39:2, New International Version.
2. Genesis 42:6*a*, Berkeley Version.
3. Genesis 45:8*a*, New International Version.
4. Genesis 50:21*a*, New International Version.
5. Genesis 50:24, New International Version.
6. Mark 14:36, Berkeley Version.
7. I am indebted for the discussion in the remainder of this section to John Fieldsend. See Fieldsend, J. (1997). "The Cup of Blessing." *Encounter with God*, March 22, p. 101; "Make Prayer Real." *Encounter with God*, March 23, p. 102.
8. See Luke 22:20.
9. See 1 Corinthians 10:16.
10. Mark 14:25, New International Version.
11. Psalm 137:1–4, Amplified Bible.
12. See Luke 23:39–41.
13. Psalm 106:4–5 gives full expression to the thief's request. See Spurgeon, C. (1993). *Psalms: Volume II*. Wheaton, IL: Crossway Books. In Spurgeon's words, "Insignificant as I am, do not forget me. Think of me with kindness, just as thou thinkest of thine own elect. I cannot ask for more, nor would I seek less. Treat me as the least of thy saints are treated and I am content. [This] is a sweet prayer, at once humble and aspiring, submissive and expansive; it might be used by a dying thief or a living apostle" (p. 98).
14. See Exodus 4:2.
15. Matthew 27:46, New International Version.

THREE
Uncovering the Neurotic Organization

1. See Kets de Vries, M.F.R., & Miller, D. (1984). *The Neurotic Organization: Diagnosing and Revitalizing Unhealthy Companies.* San Francisco: Jossey-Bass; Kets de Vries, M.F.R., & Miller, D. (1987). *Unstable at the Top: Inside the Troubled Organization.* New York: New American Library; Kets de Vries, M.F.R., & Associates (1991). *Organizations on the Couch: Clinical Perspectives on Organizational Behavior and Change.* San Francisco: Jossey-Bass. I am indebted for the discussion in the next three sections to these resources.
2. I am indebted for the description of the bureaucratic mentality to Peter Block. See Block, P. (1991). *The Empowered Manager: Positive Political Skills at Work.* San Francisco: Jossey-Bass. I have slightly modified the names of the first two parts of the description.
3. I am indebted for the discussion in the remainder of this section to Rollo May. See May, R. (1972). *Power and Innocence: A Search for the Source of Violence.* New York: W. W. Norton.
4. I am indebted for this presentation of a test for the neurotic organization to Manfred Kets de Vries and Danny Miller.

FOUR
Unraveling the Addictive Organization

1. See Matthew 7:15.
2. See Schaef, A. W., & Fassel, D. (1988). *The Addictive Organization.* San Francisco: Harper & Row.
3. I am indebted for the discussions of addictive processes and workaholism to Anne Wilson Schaef and Diane Fassel. I have changed or slightly modified the names of process numbers one, five, six and seven, and I have added number two.
4. Wallis, J. (1977). Editorial. *Sojourners,* August, pp. 6–7.
5. Schaef and Fassel, p. 120.
6. *Ibid.*, p. 132.
7. I am indebted for this presentation of a test for the addictive organization to Schaef and Fassel.
8. I am indebted for this presentation of a test for personality characteristics to Schaef and Fassel.
9. For further reading, see Beattie, M. (1987). *Codependent No More: How to Stop Controlling Others and Start Caring for Yourself.* San Francisco: HarperCollins; Hemfelt, R., Minirth, F., & Meier, P. (1989). *Love Is a Choice: Recovery for Codependent Relationships.* Nashville:

Thomas Nelson; Leman, K. (1987). *The Pleasers: Women Who Can't Say No and the Men Who Control Them*. Tarrytown, NY: Fleming H. Revell; LeSourd, N. (1991). *No Longer the Hero: The Personal Pilgrimage of an Adult Child*. Nashville: Thomas Nelson; McConnell, P. (1986). *Adult Children of Alcoholics: A Workbook for Healing*. San Francisco: Harper & Row; Mellody, P., & Miller, A. W. (1989). *Breaking Free: A Recovery Workbook for Facing Codependence*. San Francisco: Harper & Row; Wilson, S. D. (1990). *Released from Shame: Recovery for Adult Children of Dysfunctional Families*. Downers Grove, IL: InterVarsity; Woititz, J.G. (1987). *Home Away from Home: The Art of Self-Sabotage*. Pompano Beach, FL: Health Communications.

FIVE
Unmasking the Spiritually Abusive Organization

1. Matthew 7:15, Revised Standard Version.
2. Acts 20:29–30, New International Version.
3. Ezekiel 22:27, New International Version.
4. Ezekiel 34:18–19, New International Version.
5. Johnson, D., & VanVonderen, J. (1991). *The Subtle Power of Spiritual Abuse*. Minneapolis: Bethany House. P. 23.
6. Matthew 9:36, New International Version; Berkeley Version.
7. I am indebted for this discussion of characteristics of spiritual abuse to David Johnson and Jeff VanVonderen. I have slightly modified the name of number seven.
8. *Ibid.*, p. 171.
9. *Ibid.*, p. 64.
10. *Ibid.*, p. 66.
11. *Ibid.*, pp. 73–74.
12. See Arterburn, S., & Felton, J. (1991). *Toxic Faith: Understanding and Overcoming Religious Addiction*. Nashville: Thomas Nelson.
13. I am indebted for this presentation of a test for the spiritually abusive organization to Johnson and VanVonderen, especially items 2-11.
14. I am indebted for this presentation of a test for personality characteristics to Johnson and VanVonderen.
15. I am indebted for the following discussion to Tom White. See White, T. (1993). *Breaking Strongholds: How Spiritual Warfare Sets Captives Free*. Ann Arbor, MI: Servant.
16. *Ibid.*, p. 24.
17. *Ibid.*, p. 40.

18. *Ibid.*, p. 50. I have numbered the items and have changed "I" to "you," and "my" to "your."
19. I recommend White's book most highly. A thorough reading and consulting of his bibliography should get you well down the road to recovery.
20. Ezekiel 34:30–31, Revised Standard Version.

SIX
Doing a Biblical Reality Check—Part I

1. See Psalm 137:1–4.
2. The following story of Wayne Alderson is abridged from Sproul, R. C. (1980). *Stronger than Steel: The Wayne Alderson Story.* San Francisco: Harper & Row.
3. See Deuteronomy 6:23.
4. 1 Corinthians 1:9, New International Version.
5. Romans 1:1–7, Revised Standard Version.
6. See Hebrews 3:1.
7. See 2 Timothy 1:9.
8. Ephesians 4:1, King James Version.
9. Ephesians 4:1, New International Version.
10. Ephesians 4:2–6, New International Version.
11. 2 Kings 4:38–41, Berkeley Version.
12. I am indebted for the discussion in this paragraph to Marshall Sashkin. See Sashkin, M. (1986). "Participative Management Remains an Ethical Imperative." *Organizational Dynamics*, Spring, pp. 62–75.
13. Schaef and Fassel, p. 17.
14. See John 14:6.
15. I am indebted for this discussion of ideas regarding the ideal organization to Peter Block and to Peter Senge (see Senge, P. M. [1990]. *The Fifth Discipline: The Art and Practice of the Learning Organization*. New York: Doubleday). I have added number seven.
16. Colossians 2:6–7, Amplified Bible.

SEVEN
Doing a Biblical Reality Check—Part II

1. 1 Corinthians 9:19, The Living Bible.
2. Galatians 5:13, Revised Standard Version.
3. Isaiah 42:1–3, The Living Bible.
4. See Matthew 12:18–20.

5. Jeremiah 6:13–14, Berkeley Version.
6. See Psalm 78:72.
7. Proverbs 12:15, Berkeley Version.
8. Proverbs 18:13, The Living Bible.
9. John 7:51, Jerusalem Bible.
10. See 2 Corinthians 4:2.
11. 2 Timothy 2:24–25, Phillips Modern English.
12. Ezekiel 34:1–2, 4, Berkeley Version.
13. 1 Samuel 30:24, Berkeley Version.
14. See 2 Corinthians 8:15.
15. Bonhoeffer, D. (1954). *Life Together*, trans. John W. Doberstein. New York: Harper & Row. P. 108.
16. *Ibid.*, p. 99.
17. *Ibid.*, pp. 108–109.
18. See Hobbs, W. C. (1974). "On the Necessity and Feasibility of Conflict among Christian Faculty." *Christian Scholar's Review*, 4, pp. 134–139.
19. Bennis, p. 133.
20. I am indebted for the distinction between unity and unanimity to Daniel Taylor. See Taylor, D. (1986). *The Myth of Certainty: The Reflective Christian and the Risk of Commitment.* Waco: Word.
21. *Ibid.*, pp. 36–37.
22. I am indebted for the discussions of the management mentality and grieving to Walter Brueggemann. See Brueggemann, W. (1978). *The Prophetic Imagination.* Philadelphia: Fortress.
23. *Ibid.*, p. 22.
24. *Ibid.*, p. 88.
25. *Ibid.*, p. 21.
26. *Ibid.*, p. 20.
27. The following story of the Scott Bader Company is abridged from Schumacher, E. F. (1973). *Small Is Beautiful: Economics as if People Mattered.* London: Harper & Row.
28. 2 Corinthians 8:15, New International Version.
29. See Ezekiel 16:49.
30. Finnerty, A. D. (1997). *No More Plastic Jesus: Global Justice and Christian Lifestyle.* Maryknoll, NY: Orbis Books. Pp. 172–173.
31. Philippians 2:4, New International Version.
32. I am indebted for this discussion of three areas of self-sacrifice to Henri Nouwen. See Nouwen, H. J. M. (1989). *In the Name of Jesus: Reflections on Christian Leadership.* New York: Crossroad.

33. *Ibid.*, pp. 59–60.
34. John 21:18, Jerusalem Bible.
35. I am indebted for the discussion in this paragraph to James MacGregor Burns. See Burns, J. M. (1978). *Leadership*. New York: Harper & Row.
36. Verses from the Berkeley Version.
37. I am indebted for this discussion of hospitality to Henri Nouwen. See Nouwen, H. J. M. (1975). *Reaching Out: The Three Movements of the Spiritual Life*. New York: Doubleday.
38. *Ibid.*, p. 103.
39. *Ibid.*, p. 102.
40. *Ibid.*, pp. 98–99.
41. 1 John 1:1, New International Version.

EIGHT

Ministering to Others

1. Psalm 137:4, Amplified Bible.
2. I am indebted for the following discussion to Henri Nouwen (see Nouwen, H. J. M. [1972]. *The Wounded Healer: Ministry in Contemporary Society*. Garden City, NY: Doubleday). I have changed the name of the first of the three characteristics of the wounded healer.
3. Edwards, G. (1980). *A Tale of Three Kings: A Study in Brokenness*. Auburn, ME: Christian Books. Pp. 11–15, 17–18, 21–23.
4. Nouwen, *The Wounded Healer*, p. 88.
5. *Ibid.*, p. 92.
6. I am indebted for this discussion of suffering to Philip Yancey. See Yancey, P. (1988). "How Not to Spell Relief." *Christianity Today*, February 19, p. 64. I have slightly modified the names of stages one and two and have changed the name of stage five.
7. Foster, R. J. (1978). *Celebration of Discipline. The Path to Spiritual Growth*. New York: Harper & Row. P. 166.

NINE

Making Changes

1. I am indebted for the following listing of questions to Johnson and VanVonderen. Numbers 1-11 are restated and applied more specifically in chapter 10.
2. I am indebted for this discussion of the identification and redemption of the Powers to Hendrik Berkhof. See Berkhof, H. (1962). *Christ and the Powers*, trans. John H. Yoder. Scottdale, PA: Herald.

3. See Proverbs 26:11.
4. Berkhof, p. 30.
5. *Ibid.*, pp. 48–49.
6. I am indebted for the discussion of the three steps for breaking strongholds to Tom White. The following list is a reduced and modified version of White's list of signs of "spiritual subterfuge."
7. *Ibid.*, p. 154. Quoted from Eastman, D. (1989). *Love on Its Knees.* Tarrytown, NY: Chosen Books. P. 65.
8. *Ibid.*, p. 156.
9. I am indebted for the following procedure to Terry Walling and Gary Reinecke. See Walling, T. B., & Reinecke, G. B. (1996). *Refocusing Your Church: Phase Two of the Refocusing Network System.* Carol Stream, IL: ChurchSmart Resources. I have changed their brief designations and have modified their suggestions for each of the three steps.
10. White, p. 129.
11. Kilmann, R. H. (1984). *Beyond the Quick Fix: Managing Five Tracks to Organizational Success.* San Francisco: Jossey-Bass. P. 48.
12. I am indebted for this discussion of five types of coworkers to Peter Block.
13. I am indebted for the following procedure to Ralph Kilmann. I have shortened and rearranged his recommended list of steps.

TEN
Moving On

1. 1 Kings 12:16, New International Version.
2. Matthew 10:14, New International Version.
3. I am indebted for the discussion of exit and voice to Albert Hirschman. See Hirschman, A. O. (1970). *Exit, Voice, and Loyalty: Responses to Decline in Firms, Organizations and States.* Cambridge, MA: Harvard University.
4. *Ibid.*, p. 78.
5. *Ibid.*, p. 117.
6. See Morin, W. J., & Cabrera, J.C. (1991). *Parting Company: How to Survive the Loss of a Job and Find Another Successfully.* New York: Harcourt Brace Jovanovich. I have reproduced the names of their seven danger signs without change.
7. Gibran, K. (1970). *The Prophet.* New York: Alfred A. Knopf. P. 28.

8. See Johnson and VanVonderen, *The Subtle Power of Spiritual Abuse*. I have slightly modified the names of their guideline numbers one, six, seven and ten.
9. *Ibid.*, p. 220.
10. Schaef and Fassel, p. 209.
11. Lindsay, C. P., & Pasquali, J. M. (1993). "The Wounded Feminine: From Organizational Abuse to Personal Healing." *Business Horizons*, March–April, p. 39.
12. Morin and Cabrera, p. 35.
13. See Bolles, R. N. (1997). *What Color Is Your Parachute?* Berkeley: Ten Speed; Farnsworth, K. E., & Lawhead, W. H. (1981). *Life Planning: A Christian Approach to Careers*. Downers Grove, IL: InterVarsity; Gale, B., & Gale, L. (1989). *Stay or Leave*. New York: Harper & Row; Holloway, D., & Bishop, N. (1990). *Before You Say "I Quit!": A Guide to Making Successful Job Transitions*. New York: Macmillan; Morin and Cabrera, *Parting Company*.
14. See Blackaby, H. T., & King, C.V. (1994). *Experiencing God: How to Live the Full Adventure of Knowing and Doing the Will of God*. Nashville: Broadman & Holman.
15. I am indebted for the following procedure to Terry Walling. See Walling, T. B. (1996). *Perspective: Personal Time-Line*. Carol Stream, IL: ChurchSmart Resources. I have significantly shortened and simplified his recommended process.
16. I am indebted for this conception of a personal mission statement and for the procedure in the following paragraph to Terry Walling. See Walling, T. B. (1996). *Focus: Personal Mission Statement*. Carol Stream, IL: ChurchSmart Resources. I have somewhat simplified his recommended process.
17. Edwards, p. 67.
18. *Ibid.*, p. 26.
19. Bennis, pp. 123–124.
20. *Time* (1981). "Don't write any letters," June 22, p. 83.

EPILOGUE

1. Deuteronomy 6:23, New American Standard Bible.
2. Galatians 5:13*b*, Revised Standard Version.

To order additional copies of:

WOUNDED WORKERS

please send $10.99 plus $3.95 shipping and handling to:

WinePress Publishing
P.O. Box 1406
Mukilteo, WA 98275

or have your credit card ready and call:

(800) 917-BOOK

ERRATA

Wounded Workers
Kirk E. Farnsworth

Page	For	Read
Page 16, line 24	They separate us	They attempt to separate us
Page 16, line 26	more than separate us	more than try to separate us
Page 56, line 17	bale	bail
Page 176, line 10	work	word